Changing Patterns

Friendship, Fellowship and Transformation

Changing Patterns: Friendship, Fellowship and Transformation illuminates the lifelong process of developing rewarding and spiritually nurturing relationships. Michael has captured the essence of the Baha'i spirit of friendship-building and develops the argument that real friendships provide the spiritual building blocks for the transformation of both the individual and society.

Healthy friendships lead to spiritual opportunities for bringing the healing Message of Baha'u'llah to humanity in a manner that will enable consolidation of a spiritual society based on true love and respect. This book enlightens us to the process of how to change the patterns of our lives as outlined by the Central Figures of the Baha'i Revelation with illuminating stories of fellowship and transformation.

Jack McCants
Retired Member,
National Spiritual Assembly
of the Baha'is of the United States

Changing Patterns

Friendship, Fellowship and Transformation

by

Michael Winger-Bearskin

New Directions Press
Texas

NEW DIRECTIONS PRESS, Publisher
4490 Eldorado Pkwy, Suite 218, McKinney, Texas
75070

© Michael Winger-Bearskin 2004
All Rights Reserved

Cover design,
Michael Winger-Bearskin

Cover Art
Mitchell Silas

Library of Congress

ISBN 0-9763391-0-2

This book is dedicated to my lifelong friend, traveler in fellowship, and partner in spiritual transformation, Charlene

Table of Contents

PREFACE 8
INTRODUCTION 10
1 ACCIDENTAL DISCOVERY 16
2 THE ROLE OF THE INDIVIDUAL 21
    The Unpleasant Commitment 22
    Be Happy 27
    Responding to the Covenant 33
3 PREPARATION 37
    Immerse Yourselves 39
    One Hour's Reflection 42
    It's Scary Out There 46
4 WHAT IS A FIRESIDE? 49
    The First Fireside 51
    The Madness and the Method 59
    The Fireside Process 62
5 MAKE MANY CONTACTS 64
    It's Even Scarier Out There Now 65
    Who's Going to do the Community's Work 68
6 SELECT A FEW 76
    The Tuning Fork 77
    Beginning the Relationship 79
    The Intimacy Exercise[41] 81
7 DEVELOP A CLOSE FRIENDSHIP 83
    This Takes Work 84
    Can I Develop This Much Happiness 86
    Now I am Really Scared! 88

8 COMPLETE CONFIDENCE 95
How long will it take? 97
How will I know? 99

9 FINALLY TEACH THE FAITH 103
The Risk and the Reward 104

10 UNTIL THEY BECOME STRONG 108
The Coach 109
The Community 112

11 TRANSFORMATION 115

APPENDIX 2 ADDITIONAL QUOTES FROM THE WRITINGS 126

REFERENCES 140

BIBLIOGRAPHY 146

Preface

Friendship is a lifelong pursuit for every healthy member of the human family. In childhood, many of us are blessed with budding friendships among who, if we are fortunate, a treasured few remain throughout the rest of our lives.

For many of us, fellowship is compartmentalized and separate from a good bit of our lives and occurs at specific times and/or during specific activities.

And, transformation comes about only through enormous effort and often with significant hardship.

Yet, no matter how limited or expansive, each of us makes friends, shares fellowship in some form and transforms our lives in some way as we travel across the blue marble that houses our lives.

I think that friendship is the most important benefit of our life after recognizing our Creator. Its blessings are more influential than we might imagine. Fellowship should be integral to every aspect of our lives and not compartmentalized. It can illuminate our creative spirit and enrich our every endeavor. And, transformation should be our goal generated from all of our life's events both positive and negative. The dynamic force of civilization demands that we change our patterns of behavior in order to survive and thrive in today's world.

As a struggling spiritual being who has been blessed with recognizing Baha'u'llah as the Mouthpiece of God for today and a member of the Baha'i Faith for over a quarter of a century, I have been intrigued by the beauty of our Faith and the difficulty of bringing the healing Message of its glorious Writings to my fellow travelers. Thus the reason for this book.

Along the way, many people have influenced me—my grandparents, parents and their brothers and sisters who gave me a childhood that was a spiritual wellspring of love and growth. My children, Annise, Amelia and Martha and my son-in-law, Jason, have provided and continue to provide me great opportunities for reflection, understanding and personal growth. To all of them, I express my heartfelt gratitude. I would like to also express my sincere appreciation to my life partner, Charlene, for her patience, encouragement, love and spiritual assistance.

Additionally, I would like to thank those who have been instrumental in the writing of this book, either directly or indirectly. Mitchell and Christine Jacobson for their editorial comments that helped shape many of the book's stories, Joseph Cosby for his creative insights, Mary Jo Wilder for encouraging me to find my voice, and to Javidukt Khadem, Nathan and Carol Rutstein, Edward and Evelyn Diliberto, Jack McCants, Glenford Mitchell, Bahereh Samadani, Dick and Jane Grover, Marguerite Sears and June and Jack Remignanti for parenting this spiritual child in his deepening love and emerging understanding of his Faith.

Michael Winger-Bearskin
McKinney, Texas
September, 2004

Introduction

I became a Bahá'í in 1972. From the moment I was privileged to recognize Bahá'u'lláh, the issue of teaching became paramount. The Fireside was the most prominent teaching activity in every Bahá'í community in which I have lived. Set up a meeting, invite a speaker, have lots of refreshments and try hard to fill the room. If we do our part, God will surely assist us and take care of the rest.

The concept of Fireside has become common in Bahá'í language—"I was on the bus and had a wonderful Fireside" "Let me tell you about the Fireside I had at the student union" "Yesterday at the market I had the most exciting Fireside" "We hold Firesides at the meeting room in the bank every Friday night and 20-30 people come every week" "I'm hosting Firesides in my home every Friday, please tell everyone to come" "Sunday mornings at the Bahá'í Center are community Firesides, please support them." Fireside has become a synonym for teaching.

This use of the word Fireside has troubled me for some time. What is a Fireside? What is not a Fireside? What do the Central Figures of the Faith say about the Fireside? Is there more to it than meets the eye? If it is the "most effective method" as Shoghi Effendi has said it was for teaching, then why haven't we had more success in our teaching work if, in fact, we are having Firesides all the time, everywhere? And, to complicate things more, the Universal House of Justice asks us to advance the process of entry by troops. I think I understand what entry by troops means, but what is this business of advancing the process? Should we have more Firesides, more often?

In science there is a maxim that goes, "insanity is doing the same experiment over and over again and expecting different results." I think that this might apply to our approach to the concept of Fireside. Rather than a mere teaching activity, I believe that the Fireside is far more profound an idea and activity than we realize. This book will explore the method of Fireside teaching from the written guidance that we have and also attempt to uncover a far more profound meaning of its intended results than merely increasing the numbers in the Bahá'i community.

The Bahá'i Faith is about community, community-building and personal transformation. Its central tenet is the principle of the oneness of mankind—"the pivot around which all the Teachings of Bahá'u'llah revolve." [1] If the Fireside activity is the best method of teaching, then it must be closely linked not only to the concept of the oneness of mankind, but also to the actualizing of the oneness of mankind. If our beloved Faith is about personal transformation and community-building, then the process of Fireside teaching must be transforming both personally and communally. The Fireside activity itself should be transformative.

Our Faith is a faith of action. Transformation is faith in action. If we are to transform ourselves and subsequently transform society, then we must look deeply into what spirituality means for today within the context of community life. And, realize that community life means the development of relationships—close and intimate relationships. Abdu'l Bahá says, "The friends of God should weave bonds of fellowship with others and show absolute love and affection towards them. These links have a deep influence on people and they will listen. When the friends sense receptivity to the Word of God, they should deliver the Message with wisdom. They must first try and remove any apprehensions in the people they teach. In fact, every one of the believers should choose one person every year and try to establish ties of friendship with him, so that all his fear would disappear. Only then, and gradually, must he teach that person. This is the best method."[2]

Abdu'l Bahá suggests not teaching until ties of friendship have been established and all fear removed first and then gradually. What a profound and exciting idea—relationships first and teaching to follow.

In contrast, often we meet a stranger, strike up an engaging conversation, get excited about the person's seeming interest in spiritual things, and immediately invite him or her to a public meeting that we call a Fireside. We introduce them to concepts that often are rather challenging, to people that can be even more challenging, and then, if they are not interested, rationalize that it is between them and God and at least we have done our part.

We should ask ourselves if this action would attract us? Is this how we became a Bahá'i? Or, were we attracted through patient and loving friendship? And what process confirmed us in our faith? Many people I speak with mention an individual or family that loved them into the Faith either while they were seeking or just after they enrolled.

The question I have asked many of the friends is whether they would invite their closest friends and relatives to one of these Fireside gatherings. Often the answer I get is, "No, they aren't ready yet" or "No, I am afraid of what might happen and it will destroy the gradual work I have done over the years," or, "I don't trust that so and so won't say something that will offend." But these same friends have no hesitation of inviting a casual acquaintance to one of these same fireside gatherings. With a new acquaintance, there is little personal risk and if nothing happens or if that individual is upset, then at least we haven't compromised a long established friendship.

But have we delivered the message with wisdom? Have we weaved bonds of fellowship and built trust? Or, have we just occasionally been fortunate enough to be a part of someone's becoming a Bahá'í in spite of our actions. Sometimes there are positive results and someone may become a Bahá'í. Unfortunately, oftentimes that becomes the justification for unwise action and a limited or faulty process.

Across the country, many Bahá'í communities feel overwhelmed with the responsibilities of the Faith. Many individuals feel overwhelmed with their responsibilities to the Faith. "I am so busy with community activities, the 3 core activities and so on. When can I have the time to also invite someone to my home when Spiritual Assembly is on Mondays, committee meetings are on Wednesdays, children's classes are on Sundays, the Bahá'í Center requires volunteers once a week, I am trying to start a study circle, and my children have school activities that I must support as well."

- I feel too busy
- I have too many activities to support
- I feel over-administered

Or, "we are doing all of these activities, public meetings, brochures, parades, community firesides, study circles, community devotional gatherings, Spiritual Assembly and committees for various community needs and we aren't growing. What is the problem?"

- Why aren't we getting results?
- Why aren't more people participating?
- Where is the rest of the community?

When the House of Justice asks us to advance the process of entry of troops, we must ask ourselves what is a process? *A process is a series of repeatable steps that yield a predictable result*. To advance the process of entry of troops is to discover what those repeatable steps are and what are the predictable results to expect. Then we must act, reflect, analyze, adjust and improve. In *The Priceless Pearl*, Ruhiyyih Khanum explains what the Guardian meant about faith, "He well knew that to have faith in God does not mean one should not use one's mind, appraise dangers, anticipate moves, make the right decisions during a crisis." [3]

We must change the patterns of our lives and our behavior in order to meet the increasing demands of our lives.

The Fireside process has been outlined and demonstrated by the Central Figures of our Faith. If we learn the Fireside lessons well, both our teaching and consolidation work will be richly rewarded. We will work with those we already have close friendships with and we will not have the difficulties of consolidation that have plagued our communities in the past. Let us discover what the fireside process involves.

The names, and sometimes the gender, of the people in the stories in this book have been changed, but the stories are as authentic as possible to the best of my knowledge, except those that are specifically stated as fictitious. Although this book's primary audience is the Bahá'í community, I believe that the lessons to be learned are universally applicable to any faith, community action group, business relationship, public service, social and economic development or in our daily activities with our neighbors and friends.

1
Accidental Discovery

Not by the force of numbers, not by the mere exposition of a set of new and noble principles, not by an organized campaign of teaching—no matter how worldwide and elaborate in its character—not even by the staunchness of our faith or the exaltation of our enthusiasm, can we ultimately hope to vindicate in the eyes of a critical and sceptical age the supreme claim of the Abha Revelation. One thing and only one thing will unfailingly and alone secure the undoubted triumph of this sacred Cause, namely, the extent to which our own inner life and private character mirror forth in their manifold aspects the splendor of those eternal principles proclaimed by Bahá'u'lláh. (Shoghi Effendi, Bahá'í Administration, pg. 66) [4]

> Once a young student of Economics was on her way to defend her Masters' Thesis. She crossed the parking lot from her car rushing to this long awaited moment. While hurrying, with a bit of anticipation and fear, she noticed in the small corner of the curb, nestled under the leaves and debris that collect curbside, a slightly crumpled dollar bill. She, excited by her luck, bent down to pick it up and found that it was, in fact, not a dollar bill, but a hundred dollar bill.

She looked around to determine if it was possible to find the owner of the bill and decided that it would be impossible. Delighted with her fortunate circumstance, she proceeded to her meeting with the Professors who so patiently and professionally guided her research and were themselves awaiting with joy, her successful thesis defense. She had spent 3 years studying, researching, writing and preparing for this day. Of course, she passed.

But this new experience of finding the hundred-dollar bill was to profoundly change her life. Following the successful defense of her thesis, she began her job hunting. She expected, and all of her professors agreed, to get a very fine job. However, the finding of the bill caused her to become more observant of the possibility of finding more money that may have fallen unnoticed onto the ground.

As she went job hunting, she also stayed alert and sure enough, each day she found money on the street, in the grass, and almost everywhere she went—a penny here, a quarter there and sometimes a paper bill of varying denominations. In fact, she began to find between five and ten dollars per day as she not only became more observant, but spent increasing hours looking for money alone.

Over the next months, she spent less and less time job hunting and more and more time looking for money. She even bought a metal detector to assist in her new work. After a couple of months, she was averaging about $500 per month—enough to augment her part-time job at the University and sustain her current life's needs. She became obsessed with her new endeavor and convinced in its efficacy. After all, the money she found was legitimate and spent just fine at the store. It was perfectly good money.

In her new method of providing for her needs, this student of great promise compromised a much larger potential, blinded by the small success of this easier process. How sad.

How often do we delight in our successes unaware of the success that could have been! Or, unwilling to reflect honestly on our limitations! Our student was seduced by the ease of finding money and turned her back on the discipline that she prepared for and was taught by her loving teachers.

Unfortunately, many of us fall into this same trap while engaged in teaching our beloved Faith. We employ all sorts of methods that yield limited, marginal success and convince ourselves that, in spite of the meager numbers, the value and loving nature of the new believers, suggests that our methods and activities are correct. Like found money, these found believers bring value to our lives and communities.

But, like our fictional student, we fail to recognize the lost potential that a more elevated process would have brought to our endeavors. She compromised a much higher paying profession in her zeal to find more money that was just lying around. We, too, compromise a much greater long-term victory by not following the clear advice and directives available in the exhaustive guidance on the subject of teaching. We compromise a greater victory and then spend enormous effort in consolidation or worse, lose the very fruit that we so cherished.

It is not that there is anything wrong with found money or found Bahá'ís. When we find money we thank God for the blessing. But we don't change our patterns of discipline and success that are based on our learning and experience. It is the same in teaching our Faith. We thank God for the bounties He bestows upon us even when we do not follow the instructions so well. We cherish and rejoice when someone finds the Faith through a media campaign, a proclamation, a dream, a news article or other avenue. But we shouldn't think that our guidance from the Central Authority of our Faith should go unheeded because of God's grace and bounties.

The process of Fireside teaching has been outlined and demonstrated by the Central Figures of our Faith and expounded upon by the beloved Guardian in numerous letters. This book will examine the process of Fireside teaching. It will focus on the Fireside method as elucidated by Abdu'l-Bahá and Shoghi Effendi and hopefully uncover the true meaning of the Fireside. In the course of this discovery, perhaps we will find that the Fireside provides for us the foundation for the transformation of the human condition—that within its process lies the very core of the development of new patterns of relationships that will, over time, completely change the society in which we live.

This book will begin with an exploration of the role of the individual in raising up a new society, examine the definition and process of Fireside teaching, link that process with the transformation in the nature of our community relationships, and, finally, provide a plan of action for individuals and communities. It is the role of the Fireside, beyond merely a teaching method, that will provide the focus for discovery in this book. Nestled in the guidance on Fireside teaching rests a far more profound concept that will uplift our human relationships and provide a recipe for transforming our individual, family and community lives.

2
The Role of the Individual

The field is indeed so immense, the period so critical, the Cause so great, the workers so few, the time so short, the privilege so priceless, that no follower of the Faith of Bahá'u'lláh, worthy to bear His name, can afford a moment's hesitation. Shoghi Effendi, <u>Advent of Divine Justice</u>, pg. 46[5]

Never before in the history of religion has the role and responsibility of the individual been so consistently and continuously promoted. At every turn and in almost every document of our Faith the role of the individual has been outlined and expounded upon. In fact, in no less weighty a statement, the House of Justice, in its Ridvan 153 letter, states, "Shoghi Effendi underscored the absolute necessity of individual initiative and action. He explained that without the support of the individual, 'at once wholehearted, continuous and generous,' every measure and plan of his National Spiritual Assembly is 'foredoomed to failure;' the purpose of the Master's Divine Plan is 'impeded;' furthermore, the sustaining strength of Bahá'u'lláh Himself 'will be withheld from every and each individual who fails in the long run to arise and play his part.' Hence, at the very crux of any progress to be made is the individual believer, who possesses the power of execution which only he can release through his own initiative and sustained action."[6]

The Unpleasant Commitment

Upon the individual rests the true transformation of society. Our individual actions will not only set the tone of our own lives, but will influence the lives of others. We are an organic entity. With our love we generate love. With our hate we further hate. With our compassion we find compassion. Abdu'l Bahá enjoined upon us the admonition to be happy. This is not the frivolous encouragement of a kind old man. This is a Commandment of God. To be happy, we must know what will lead us to happiness and what will draw us away from it. Our road to happiness depends upon the combination of our individual spiritual growth and our collective influence to change society.

A friend of mine told me the following story of how individual initiative and a true spirit of faith changed his life. He was a gifted public speaker, prominent member of the Bahá'í community in the United States and a teacher at a small college:

> Hilda was a humble, middle-aged, white woman who earned her very limited living cleaning homes of wealthy people. She suffered from narcolepsy, a syndrome that uncontrollably put her to sleep for brief periods without warning. It affected her disposition and demeanor. She shied away from any situation that would require her to speak in public. But Hilda knew that her happiness depended on her service to her Faith. She knew that her assistance from God was dependent upon her teaching the Cause.

So, she had a Fireside in her home every nineteen days in obedience to her beloved Guardian.

Hilda's personality was a bit rough on the edges, was a test for some who didn't know her very well, and often was judged on the surface of her outward being. Once, while at a Bahá'í summer school, she asked my friend, a renowned speaker, to come to her Fireside and speak with her guests. He didn't want to do it because he thought that it would be a waste of his time as he was a very busy person with many responsibilities. He also was not very attracted to Hilda. He didn't have a high regard for Hilda's ability to make his time worthwhile. After all, Hilda even fell asleep during the Hand of the Cause's talk at Green Acre!! However, he remembered a promise he made while in a prayerful moment that he would go anywhere he could, if asked to serve the Faith, during the next year.

So, he scheduled a time long into the future with the hope that something more important would come up and permit him to beg off the commitment. Time went by and the day of the Fireside came with no important event surfacing to allow him to change his commitment. That evening, however, was the beginning of the basketball championship playoffs and his favorite team was playing. He knew that the gathering at Hilda's home, more than 50 miles away, was probably going to be a waste of time. He grumbled to himself about how nobody would be there anyway and being an avid sports fan, he was going to miss a very important game that he longed to watch. He went to the phone to cancel the engagement. After all, wasn't the weather a little bad and couldn't he feel the slightest coming on of a possible cold?

But, he couldn't cancel. He knew that his own spiritual life could be hanging in the balance—he made a commitment to Bahá'u'lláh. His own love for service to his Faith demanded that he go. His ultimate happiness depended on fulfilling his promise. So, he got in his car and drove to Hilda's home.

Walking up the stairs to Hilda's humble apartment, this well-known and well-loved speaker wondered why he made a commitment that he couldn't fulfill with radiance in his heart. He admonished himself for his lack of spirituality. As he approached the door to Hilda's apartment he said a little prayer for the evening and went in.

Hilda was thrilled that he came. He was the first to arrive. She welcomed him into her apartment that she had spent the day preparing for the Fireside. She had cleaned and vacuumed the apartment, prepared modest refreshments for her guests, placed her best dishes and silverware on the table, mixed a juice drink from the can and said a prayer for God to bless her effort. Hilda, though living a humble existence, always took off work the day of her Fireside so she could prepare for her guests. Guests, friends really, that she personally invited.

After a short time, one after the other of the people that Hilda invited to her home came-- people of prominence and wealth, folks of humble origins like her, young and old, black and white. In fact the apartment filled to capacity and each soul that came showed a love and admiration for Hilda that caused the speaker to transform his own heart and realize that he was in the home of a spiritual giant. He saw with new eyes and felt with a new heart and sought God's forgiveness for thinking about breaking his commitment to come. He was humbled and inspired by what he witnessed and gave one of the best talks he had ever given and, late into the night as he lay in his own bed, he wondered where the words of that talk came from—knowing, but not knowing at the same time.

Both Hilda and the speaker were striving to change their own lives day by day while also influencing those they came in contact with. They knew that their job was to edify the souls of others and assist others to look for and contemplate the Divine. In the words of the ancient Iroquois elders, they were "following their instructions and they were well."

> Regarding the sense of inadequacy that sometimes hampers individual initiative, a letter written on his behalf conveys the Guardian's advice: "Chief among these, you mention the lack of courage and of initiative on the part of the believers, and a feeling of inferiority which prevents them from addressing the public. It is precisely these weaknesses that he wishes the friends to overcome, for these do not only paralyse their efforts but actually serve to quench the flame of faith in their hearts. Not until all the friends come to realize that every one of them is able, in his own measure, to deliver the Message, can they ever hope to reach the goal that has been set before them by a loving and wise Master.... Everyone is a potential teacher. He has only to use what God has given him and thus prove that he is faithful to his trust." The Universal House of Justice, Ridvan 153 B.E.[7]

Hilda knew her limitation as a speaker. So, she made a partnership with capable Bahá'ís and spent her time humbly making friends, building loving relationships and inviting those friends to her apartment. She knew that she could show love and compassion for others, that she could give some small service to those she came in contact with, and, that if she stayed obedient to her Guardian her life would be blessed and meaningful.

Be Happy

Our instructions for today are a continuous stream of loving directives from the Universal House of Justice. It is this responsiveness and obedience that will guarantee our happiness and allow us to follow Abdu'l Bahá's commandment, "Be happy."

> O Deaf, Hear! O Dumb, Speak! O Dead, Arise!
> Be Happy!
> Be Happy!
> Be full of Joy!
>
> This is the day of the Proclamation of the Báb! It is the Festival of the Forerunner of the Blessed Beauty (Bahá'u'lláh). It is the day of the dawning of the Morning of Guidance. Abdu'l Bahá in London, pg 127[8]
>
> May everyone point to you and ask, "Why are these people so happy?" I want you to be happy in Green Acre, to laugh, smile and rejoice in order that others may be made happy by you. I will pray for you. Abdu'l Bahá, Promulgation of Universal Peace, pg 219[9]
>
> Rest assured, persevere, and be happy.
> Your true and grateful brother,
> Shoghi[10]

Radiance of spirit, happiness, pure heart—these are the attributes that attract the interest of truth-seeking people. If we were not happy, why would anyone be attracted to us or to anything we say? If we are not happy, if we live within an air of depression or despondency, in what way can we expect others to believe that Bahá'u'lláh's healing message has transformed our lives and therefore can change theirs? This isn't to say that we do not have terrific trials and that we are not periodically unhappy or depressed. But if this is our normal manner and we go through life's trials without the spiritual acquiescence that we are enjoined to acquire, how would we influence others to walk with us in our chosen pathway.

Marjan was a student in her first week on the college campus as a full-time student. She was nervous about making friends—was she going to be successful, was she able to understand as much as the other students who would almost assuredly be older than she was? She was just barely 17. But she was raised in a loving Bahá'í home and knew that this was another opportunity to stretch herself and find ways to teach a Cause that she had just recently brought into her heart completely on her own. It was not just being an obedient daughter, but now she understood about obedience to her true Father.

Marjan had an inner calm and radiance of spirit that illumined all who met her. Although she was a beautiful young woman, her physical beauty was not what attracted others to her. Her innate compassion for others and kindness to strangers was something that she strived for in her daily prayers and that was what others responded to. Although she had her share of difficulties, she was always happy when in the company of strangers and co-workers.

In her first week at college, the school held a leadership retreat for those interested. This was right up Marjan's alley. She signed up and went off to the cabin retreat in the midst of the Finger Lakes of upstate New York. In the initial group sessions, the students were taken through a series of icebreakers and thought-provoking exercises. Marjan relied on her recent study circle of *Advent of Divine Justice* that she had co-facilitated with her father to address many of the social issues raised during the exercises.

William was taken, not only by her confidence and radiance of spirit, but by the courage of her convictions that she related during discussions. He maneuvered to be in her group as often as possible. When he asked her about where she got such penetrating ideas, she smiled, took a breath, and said, "I am a Bahá'í and these ideas come from my Faith."

Well, William didn't have a clue what that meant, but he was smitten by the glow. Over the next months, William came to know Marjan and began to fall in love with her. He had never met anyone so happy, he would say. When he came to visit her family, he noticed a very different atmosphere than what he was used to. It wasn't that he didn't have a wonderful family also, but the topics at the dinner table and the interaction between the parents and their children was very foreign to him. Marjan's father treated him with the respect of a peer and her mother overflowed with love for him, even though they didn't know him that long.

Slowly, William became attracted to the Source from where the love of Marjan and her family drew their strength. He was a struggling student and the discussions and encouragement from Marjan's family sustained him through a very rough period of studies. In fact, William was not a very good student. He understood his field from a practical point of view and did better than many of the other students on labs, but he tested poorly.

Over the next year, William began in earnest his study of the Bahá'í Teachings. He spent many free evenings at Marjan and her parents' home asking questions and discussing those things that he was interested in. He decided two things over the course of that study. One, he wanted to become a Bahá'í, but wanted to slowly bring that news to his dear parents. Second, he wanted to marry Marjan. William and Marjan gradually disclosed to William's parents his intentions. They grew to love Marjan and became friends with her parents.

One day, William's mother asked him when he planned on becoming a Bahá'í. This took him by surprise as he wasn't prepared to disclose that to her yet. But, he noticed that his mother was asking him in a very loving way and knew that she had already approved. When he asked permission to marry, both his parents joyfully embraced his choice. They were married shortly thereafter.

Although William continued to struggle with school, he had an inner confidence building in him as he attended study classes and immersed himself into the Bahá'í community. Following a long struggle, he graduated in the lower third of his class. However, his technical work became known throughout the school and when the corporations came recruiting, William was offered the highest paying job of his class and received the highest achievement award for contributions to the field by a student—he had already submitted two patent proposals in a very technical area.

Marjan's happy and loving spirit attracted a seeking soul, transformed her own life and set her on a new path of service to her Beloved. William was loved into the Faith through close friendship. By the time he became a Bahá'i, there was very little consolidation work to be done. He was ready to find his path of service to his newborn faith.

When we reflect the joy of life that Abdu'l Bahá desires for us the world around us responds. True happiness comes from the assistance of the Concourse on High responding to our immersion into the teaching work of the Faith. It is the assistance from on high that attracts the hearts of our contacts and inspires them to begin seeking. Not everyone seeks in a fervid fashion. Many hearts must be warmed by the loving attraction of a sincere relationship before they begin to inquire about those things that for most seem so distant and foreign.

> The role of the individual is of unique importance in the work of the Cause. It is the individual who manifests the vitality of faith upon which the success of the teaching work and the development of the community depend. Bahá'u'lláh's command to each believer to teach His Faith confers an inescapable responsibility which cannot be transferred to, or assumed by, any institution of the Cause. The individual alone can exercise those capacities which include the ability to take initiative, to seize opportunities, to form friendships, to interact personally with others, to build relationships, to win the cooperation of others in common service to the Faith and society, and to convert into action the decisions made by consultative bodies. It is the individual's duty to "consider every avenue of approach which he might utilize in his personal attempts to capture the attention, maintain the interest, and deepen the faith, of those whom he seeks to bring into the fold of his Faith."
> (The Universal House of Justice, Ridvan 154 B.E.) [11]

Responding to the Covenant

A covenant is an agreement between two parties wherein each obligates herself or himself to the other. Bahá'u'lláh enjoins upon His followers certain duties and obligates Himself to be with them under all circumstances. "Love Me that I may love thee" [12], suggests that the believers must make efforts to receive His love and then that love will flow to them. It is not that the divine love of God is withheld, but that in order to receive it one must orient to it. The characteristic of the sun is to shine. Whether we are oriented to it or not does not change its effulgence. However, for us to partake of its benefit, we must turn toward it as a flower or tree bends to receive its light.

Bahá'u'lláh has enjoined upon His believers to teach His Cause. Therefore, it is incumbent upon us to reflect deeply about what the injunction of teaching calls us to do.

> The Pen of the Most High hath decreed and imposed upon every one the obligation to teach this Cause.... God will, no doubt, inspire whosoever detacheth himself from all else but Him, and will cause the pure waters of wisdom and utterance to gush out and flow copiously from his heart. Verily, thy Lord, the All-Merciful, is powerful to do as He willeth, and ordaineth whatsoever He pleaseth. Bahá'u'lláh, *Gleanings*, pg 315[13]

When one contemplates the teaching obligation in one's covenant with Bahá'u'lláh, it is interesting to note that this obligation will exist throughout the Dispensation of Bahá'u'lláh, "destined to endure for no less than a thousand years." [14] Abdu'l Bahá further states that the world, "...will become a single nation. Religious and sectarian antagonism, the hostility of races and peoples, and differences among nations, will be eliminated. All men will adhere to one religion, will have one common faith, will be blended into one race, and become a single people. All will dwell in one common fatherland, which is the planet itself." [15]

With this in mind, why would teaching be obligated throughout the length of the Dispensation—perhaps long after the world and its peoples acknowledge their collective belief in Bahá'u'lláh?

Bahá'u'lláh tells us that teaching is the "exaltation of the Word of God." [16] It is not to be merely understood in terms of numbers, conversions and proclamations. "Think not that We have revealed unto you a mere code of laws. Nay, rather, We have unsealed the choice Wine with the fingers of might and power," [17] is His emphatic pronouncement. Therefore teaching must be viewed in a much broader context and its application must be contemplated with profound depth.

In our covenant with Bahá'u'lláh, we must bear in mind that teaching is a prerequisite to Divine assistance. "Exaltation of the Word of God" challenges our daily behavior and provides insight into our human relations. When engaged in teaching, we begin re-inventing our actions and aligning them with the Covenant of God.

> It is clear that in this day, confirmations from the unseen world are encompassing all those who deliver the divine Message. Should the work of teaching lapse, these confirmations would be entirely cut off, since it is impossible for the loved ones of God to receive assistance unless they teach.
>
> ("Selections from the Writings of 'Abdu'l-Bahá, sec. 209, pp. 264) [18]

When not engaged in the process of teaching or delivering the divine Message, we cannot transform our lives and bring ourselves into alignment with the Covenant of Bahá'u'lláh. Of course the delivery of the divine Message can take numerous forms and implies neither a particular method nor a specific set of actions.

> Shoghi Effendi underscored the absolute necessity of individual initiative and action. He explained that without the support of the individual, "at once wholehearted, continuous and generous," every measure and plan of his National Spiritual Assembly is "foredoomed to failure," the purpose of the Master's Divine Plan is "impeded"; furthermore, the sustaining strength of Bahá'u'lláh Himself "will be withheld from every and each individual who fails in the long run to arise and play his part."

Hence, at the very crux of any progress to be made is the individual believer, who possesses the power of execution which only he can release through his own initiative and sustained action..."

(The Universal House of Justice, Ridvan 153 B.E. (World)) [19]

Upon the efforts in teaching, or exalting the Word of God, depends the individual's spiritual growth. The many and varied forms that this can take is between the individual and his or her Lord. Some will take the direct route and others the indirect. Others will, as they grow and mature, use both as necessary. Exalting the Word of God also encompasses the teaching we do within the Bahá'i community as well—children, youth and adults.

3
Preparation

To strive to obtain a more adequate understanding of the significance of 'Bahá'u'lláh's stupendous Revelation must, it is my unalterable conviction, remain the first obligation and the object of the constant endeavor of each one of its loyal adherents. An exact and thorough comprehension of so vast a system, so sublime a revelation, so sacred a trust, is for obvious reasons beyond the reach and ken of our finite minds. We can, however, and it is our bounden duty to seek to derive fresh inspiration and added sustenance as we labor for the propagation of His Faith through a clearer apprehension of the truths it enshrines and the principles on which it is based. Shoghi Effendi, <u>World Order of Bahá'u'lláh</u>, pg 100[20]

To prepare oneself for the field of teaching is like the preparation one would make to meet his heart's delight. Full of love, longing to please, no amount of effort would seem too burdensome. A joy of discovery and anticipation must accompany this journey.

Of course, there is always a balance between preparation and action. In fact, action is part of the process of preparation. We could spend endless hours studying how to swim or how to ride a bicycle, but not until we put into action through practice and trial can we truly learn and become successful. An important aspect of learning how to do anything, involves reflection and analysis. If we can recall when we learned how to ride a bicycle, we made many mistakes and spent not an inconsiderable amount of time adjusting and adjusting until we finally got it right. It is the same with teaching. There is a saying that practice makes perfect. But, incorrect practice without reflection and analysis only confirms incorrect action and makes it habitual. In order to learn, we must take action, reflect on the outcome of that action, analyze what was good and what was not good and adjust.

> To optimize the use of these capacities, the individual draws upon his love for Bahá'u'lláh, the power of the Covenant, the dynamics of prayer, the inspiration and education derived from regular reading and study of the Holy Texts, and the transformative forces that operate upon his soul as he strives to behave in accordance with the divine laws and principles. In addition to these, the individual, having been given the duty to teach the Cause, is endowed with the capacity to attract particular blessings promised by Bahá'u'lláh. "Whoso openeth his lips in this Day," the Blessed Beauty asserts, "and maketh mention of the name of his Lord, the hosts of Divine inspiration shall descend upon him from the heaven of My name, the All-Knowing, the All-Wise. On him shall also descend the Concourse on high, each bearing aloft a chalice of pure light."

...In so responding, each individual, too, must make a conscious decision as to what he or she will do to serve the Plan, and as to how, where and when to do it. This determination enables the individual to check the progress of his actions and, if necessary, to modify the steps being taken. Becoming accustomed to such a procedure of systematic striving lends meaning and fulfilment to the life of any Bahá'í.

(The Universal House of Justice, Ridvan 155 B.E.) [21]

Immerse Yourselves

Bahá'u'lláh enjoins upon us to "Immerse yourselves in the ocean of My words, that ye may unravel its secrets, and discover all the pearls of wisdom that lie hid in its depths." [22] Immersion requires involvement and getting in over our head. The immersion process implies action. Living the Bahá'í life requires conscious knowledge acted upon. Its Teachings encourage action, reflection and adjustment—and more action.

> George became a Bahá'í almost 30 years ago, almost on his own. He casually met a couple of Bahá'ís along the way, but it was his own perseverance and study that brought him to acknowledge his belief in Bahá'u'lláh. However, once he became a Bahá'í, it was the constant immersion in the Writings with the help of a loving and dedicated family that truly changed his life.

Charles and Margaret and their six children were recently returned from a pioneering post for several years in South America. Their home was a center of activity and bustling with people, food, and discussion. George came to Charles and Margaret's home every day to visit for almost a year after he became a Bahá'í. He was challenged by the vibrancy of the discussion and the love of Charles and Margaret. He had many questions as he read the numerous books that he purchased. The family answered his questions, gave him encouragement and "patiently, tactfully, yet determinedly" loved him into full acceptance of whatever was part of his newly awakening Faith.

About a month after George was enrolled into the Faith, Charles invited him to give a talk at a public meeting held each month at a room in a local bank. George was terrified, but was so encouraged by both Charles and Margaret that he said he would try. The night of the meeting came and the room slowly filled with about 10 people. George had prepared by practicing with Charles and launched into his short prepared talk. During the questions and answer portion, he slowly discovered that all of the people who had come were Bahá'ís, but they still asked questions that they were interested in and George became a facilitator for the discussion—asking others what they thought was the answer and guiding everyone to the books that he had brought with him for the answers just as Charles had taught him to do by his example.

George learned a lesson in how to prepare one's self for teaching. He discovered that immersing himself into the work of the Faith brought more understanding and courage. He was excited about the possibility of actually learning how to teach—something that had really scared him before.

Over the years, George kept immersing himself into the teaching arena. He tried every method that came along. Some methods he didn't like, but he tried until after many years, George says that he now feels confident about teaching and knows what he is good at and what he doesn't like. George and his wife, Cathy, no longer join every teaching activity. They have discovered that making long and enduring friends gives them great satisfaction and also provides a way to teach that is natural, loving and with little need for formal consolidation.

They have a Fireside in their home almost every week, but you probably wouldn't notice it unless they told you about it. Their home is always open to their friends with the intent of bringing the healing Message of Bahá'u'lláh to them by showing a loving Bahá'í home and warm hospitality. When conversation turns to current events, family difficulties or whatever, they provide a Bahá'í perspective when appropriate and gradually over time, their friends ask more and more and sometimes begin searching the Writings to find their own way into the Faith.

When we immerse ourselves in the action of the Faith, we bathe our entire being in the warmth of the Cause. Teaching shouldn't be something that we do outside of our normal activities. Our activities should be normalized into the process of teaching. What I mean is, we should not be schizophrenic in our lives. Our lives shouldn't be compartmentalized into Bahá'í and not-Bahá'í activities. Our lives can be spiritualized and look normal to others with a twist of happiness that emanates from our connection to Baha'u'llah. Speaking about our Faith can be a normal part of our lives and not an event that must be scheduled.

One Hour's Reflection

Many years ago I was at a gathering with the Hand of the Cause of God, Mr. Faizi. Someone asked him about meditation. At the time there were various methods circulating around the Bahá'í community with different schools of thought and practices being touted as the preferred method or "very Bahá'í-like" or "Bahá'í-inspired." Mr. Faizi said simply that, in his opinion, meditation was the action that one took following prayerful contemplation and inspiration. That true meditation was the spiritualized actions we take in carrying out the directives of the Faith. How different than the practiced methods that require one to sit idly and cast out all thoughts and "clear our minds." For the Bahá'i, the religious experience involves action, individual initiative and personal responsibility.

Although Mr. Faizi emphasized action, the process of reflection plays a key role in refining and altering our behavior. Bahá'u'lláh states, "One hour's reflection is preferable to seventy years pious worship." [23] The process of reflection requires us to bring ourselves "into account each day."[24] It elevates our thinking to consider what we do well, what we need to work on, who we have interacted with, and are we meeting our personal and spiritual goals and expectations.

True reflection does not mean just meditation. Sometimes it involves getting information from others, consultation and then prayerful meditation and contemplation. Above all, it suggests that we must be truthful and dispassionate.

> Truthfulness is the foundation of all human virtues. Without truthfulness, progress and success, in all the worlds of God, are impossible for any soul. When this holy attribute is established in man, all the divine qualities will also be acquired.
>
> (Abdu'l Bahá, LSA Guidelines)[25]

Being truthful with ourselves is perhaps the most important and most difficult discipline we can learn. It requires reflection, objectivity and true humility. Without it, not only can we not progress as Abdu'l Bahá asserts, but we will be debilitated in our process of improving and perfecting our actions. Imagine a performer or athlete or teacher who cannot recognize or admit to actions that limit his or her success! Even great singers or athletes use a coach to assist in their process of reflection and the refinement of their craft. They solicit information and then reflect and alter their actions for improvement. Yet often in our teaching work, we neither solicit feedback, nor analyze our actions, nor reflect deeply on the outcome of our behavior. Often, we satisfy ourselves with limited responses and leave the outcome to God believing that it is not in our power to affect a better result. Certainly the ultimate outcome is between a seeker and his Lord, but our actions can lead to one's uncovering and discovering the Faith of Bahá'u'lláh. If we are not getting the results we want, we cannot expect improvement by doing the same things over and over again in the same way.

> To optimize the use of these capacities, the individual draws upon his love for Bahá'u'lláh, the power of the Covenant, the dynamics of prayer, the inspiration and education derived from regular reading and study of the Holy Texts, and the transformative forces that operate upon his soul as he strives to behave in accordance with the divine laws and principles. In addition to these, the individual, having been given the duty to teach the Cause, is endowed with the capacity to attract particular blessings promised by Bahá'u'lláh. "Whoso openeth his lips in this Day," the Blessed Beauty asserts, "and maketh mention of the

name of his Lord, the hosts of Divine inspiration shall descend upon him from the heaven of My name, the All-Knowing, the All-Wise. On him shall also descend the Concourse on high, each bearing aloft a chalice of pure light."

...In so responding, each individual, too, must make a conscious decision as to what he or she will do to serve the Plan, and as to how, where and when to do it. This determination enables the individual to check the progress of his actions and, if necessary, to modify the steps being taken. Becoming accustomed to such a procedure of systematic striving lends meaning and fulfilment to the life of any Bahá'í.

(The Universal House of Justice, Ridvan 155 B.E.)[26]

The very act of striving or struggling or endeavoring suggests movement, analysis, reflection and determination to improve. We check the progress of our actions by reflection, analysis and consultation and then modify for improvement when necessary. The acts of reflection, analysis, consultation and modification are at the core of the advancement of the process of entry by troops in which the House of Justice encourages us to fully participate.

It's Scary Out There

Ronald lived and worked in Europe for a large American multi-national company. He wasn't interested in religion or spiritual knowledge. He was a very pragmatic engineer dedicated to providing skillful and expert work for his employer. Until, of course, he met Sabrina, another employee at his company and his future wife. Sabrina was a Bahá'í from a small town in Germany. Sabrina's experience in the Faith was one of very intimate friendships with her fellow Bahá'ís and an approach to teaching that was very conservative by American standards and based on building relationships. Sabrina could never imagine introducing the Faith to a stranger with whom she had no relationship.

Not long after they were dating, Ronald became more and more attracted to Sabrina and what motivated her life. He began a systematic study of her faith and began to learn how it affected her life. His own Jewish religious experience was fine as a child, but it did not hold much interest for him as an adult. He became more and more attracted to the teachings of the Bahá'í Faith. In fact, because of his interest in the Faith, his understanding of his Jewish heritage came more into focus and he understood it with a far greater capacity.

Soon they were married. Ronald became a Bahá'í soon after that and then he was transferred back to America. Sabrina joined Ronald in New York and had to learn to speak English.

Sabrina and Ronald became active in their Bahá'í community, but were often shocked and dismayed by the teaching activities that they experienced. Direct teaching, proclamations, large public gatherings, debates and other methods were at odds with their personal sensitivities. After one particular Fireside where they watched a lone seeker answer a barrage of questions and listen to an overwhelming response from 10 to 15 Bahá'ís, they decided to investigate more fully the Writings of the Faith for specific guidance as to how to teach the Faith. They determined that they would not duplicate that experience in their own desire to teach the healing Message of Bahá'u'lláh.

Fortunately Ronald and Sabrina were deepened in their love and devotion to Bahá'u'lláh. Without a mature understanding of who Bahá'u'lláh is they may have become disillusioned and alienated from the Bahá'í community. The idea of teaching directly was very scary to them. The only models they saw seemed ineffective and unattractive. But they knew that the Guardian had said that both the direct and indirect methods were necessary.

So, they determined to find out what the criteria for teaching entailed.

A friend of Ronald and Sabrina encouraged them to study the book, *Advent of Divine Justice* by Shoghi Effendi. From that they learned the true meaning of teaching and the spiritual prerequisites necessary for success. They began to carry out the suggestions and directives from the Guardian. They have slowly and methodically altered their approach and have become effective in their teaching endeavors. Ronald and Sabrina have learned that friendship-making and relationship-building are the most effective means to bring people to the recognition of the transformational effect of the Writings of Bahá'u'lláh.

Ronald and Sabrina have learned what so many of us are learning—that the Faith of Bahá'u'lláh will transform the individual, the community and the world. Its influence will rearrange the affairs of the world by changing how we build relationships, how we develop intimate and close friendships and how we interact on a daily basis with everyone we meet. The dynamic forces at work in the world today provide opportunities at every juncture to bring spiritual relief to a moribund society—a society wracked by ever-increasing crises that continue to buffet time-honored institutions everywhere. We must provide an oasis of loving and sincere friendships in the midst of a horrific spiritual desert. In this way, people will be attracted to us and to the Source of our happiness.

What is a Fireside?

The friends of God should weave bonds of fellowship with others and show absolute love and affection towards them. These links have a deep influence on people and they will listen. When the friends sense receptivity to the Word of God, they should deliver the Message with wisdom. They must first try and remove any apprehensions in the people they teach. In fact, every one of the believers should choose one person every year and try to establish ties of friendship with him, so that all his fear would disappear. Only then, and gradually, must he teach that person. This is the best method. 'Abdu'l-Bahá, From a Tablet- translated from the Persian[27]

A Fireside is a method of teaching. It is not the only method and should not be confused with teaching in general. We should be encouraged to employ many methods and paths to teaching. However, it is important to understand that not all teaching is a Fireside and that the Fireside has been identified and spoken of by the Master and the Guardian in very specific terms.

First of all, the Fireside is a small gathering held in one's home. If it is held in a public place, it is not a Fireside. It is a public meeting that is still a viable teaching activity. A Fireside is an intimate gathering that does not require a speaker, although there is nothing wrong with having a designated speaker and topic. It is an event where Bahá'ís can show hospitality and provide an atmosphere where one feels safe and secure. It is an activity that first and foremost encourages friendships. It can and should be a natural extension of our lives, not an event that is separate.

> The most effective method of teaching is the Fireside group, where new people can be shown Bahá'í hospitality, and ask all questions which bother them. They can feel there the true Bahá'í spirit—and it is the spirit that quickeneth.
>
> (From a letter dated 20 October 1956 written on behalf of Shoghi Effendi to an individual believer)[28]

> The Guardian hopes the Friends ... will display the loving spirit of the Master in their contacts, and then win those souls to the Faith. The Fireside method of teaching seems to produce the greatest results, when each one invites friends into their homes once in nineteen days, and introduces them to the Faith. Close association and loving service affects the hearts; and when the heart is affected, then the spirit can enter. It is the Holy Spirit that quickens, and the Friends must become channels for its diffusion.
>
> (From a letter dated 27 January 1957 written on behalf of Shoghi Effendi to an individual believer)[29]

The First Fireside

The first seeker of our Faith prepared himself and embarked upon a journey to find the Promised One of all ages. Mulla Husayn traveled to Shiraz, Persia in that fateful spring of 1844. Upon his arrival in Shiraz, he was met by a Youth of serene beauty who invited him to His home. After serving tea and making His guest comfortable, the Youth asked Mulla Husayn why he was in Shiraz. The following is from the recollection of Mulla Husayn from *The Dawnbreakers*:

> 'The Youth who met me outside the gate of Shiraz overwhelmed me with expressions of affection and loving-kindness. He extended to me a warm invitation to visit His home, and there refresh myself after the fatigues of my journey. I prayed to be excused, pleading that my two companions had already arrived for my stay in that city, and were now awaiting my return. "Commit them to the care of God," was His reply; "He will surely protect and watch over them." Having spoken these words, He bade me follow Him. I was profoundly impressed by the gentle yet compelling manner in which that strange Youth spoke to me. As I followed Him, His gait, the charm of His voice, the dignity of His bearing, served to enhance my first impressions of this unexpected meeting.
>
> "'We soon found ourselves standing at the gate of a house of modest appearance. He knocked at the door, which was soon opened

by an Ethiopian servant. "Enter therein in peace, secure," were His words as He crossed the threshold and motioned me to follow Him. His invitation, uttered with power and majesty, penetrated my soul. I thought it a good augury to be addressed in such words, standing as I did on the threshold of the first house I was entering in Shiraz, a city the very atmosphere of which had produced already an indescribable impression upon me. Might not my visit to this house, I thought to myself, enable me to draw nearer to the Object of my quest? Might it not hasten the termination of a period of intense longing, of strenuous search, of increasing anxiety, which such a quest involves? As I entered the house and followed my Host to His chamber, a feeling of unutterable joy invaded my being. Immediately we were seated, He ordered a ewer of water to be brought, and bade me wash away from my hands and feet the stains of travel. I pleaded permission to retire from His presence and perform my ablutions in an adjoining room. He refused to grant my request, and proceeded to pour the water over my hands. He then gave me to drink of a refreshing beverage, after which He asked for the samovar and Himself prepared the tea which He offered me.

"'Overwhelmed with His acts of extreme kindness, I arose to depart. "The time for evening prayer is approaching," I ventured to observe. "I have promised my friends to join them at that hour in the Masjid-i-Ilkhani." With extreme courtesy and calm He replied: "You must surely have made the hour of your return conditional upon the will and pleasure of God. It seems that His will has decreed otherwise. You need have no fear of having broken your pledge." His dignity and self-assurance silenced me. I renewed my ablutions and prepared for prayer. He, too, stood beside me and prayed. Whilst praying, I unburdened my soul, which was much oppressed, both by the mystery of this interview and the strain and stress of my search. I breathed this prayer: "I have striven with all my soul, O my God, and until now have failed to find Thy promised Messenger. I testify that Thy word faileth not, and that Thy promise is sure."

"'That night, that memorable night, was the eve preceding the fifth day of Jamadiyu'l-Avval, in the year 1260 A.H. It was about an hour after sunset when my youthful Host began to converse with me. "Whom, after Siyyid Kazim," He asked me, "do you regard as his successor and your leader?" "At the hour of his death," I replied, "our departed teacher insistently exhorted us to forsake our homes, to scatter far and wide, in quest of the promised Beloved. I have, accordingly, journeyed to Persia, have arisen to accomplish his will, and am still engaged in my quest." "Has your teacher," He further enquired, "given you any detailed indications as to the distinguishing features of the promised One?" "Yes," I replied, "He is of a pure lineage, is of illustrious descent, and of the seed of Fatimih. As to His age, He is more than twenty and less than thirty. He is endowed with innate knowledge. He is of medium height, abstains from smoking, and is free from bodily deficiency." He paused for a while and then with vibrant voice declared: "Behold, all these signs are manifest in Me!" He then considered each of the above-mentioned signs separately, and conclusively demonstrated that each and all were applicable to His person. I was greatly surprised, and politely observed: "He whose advent we await is a Man of unsurpassed holiness, and the Cause He is to reveal, a Cause of tremendous power. Many and diverse are the requirements which He who claims to be its visible embodiment must needs fulfil. How often has Siyyid Kazim referred to the vastness of the knowledge of the promised One! How often did he say: 'My own knowledge is but a drop compared with that with which He has been endowed. All my attainments are but a speck of dust in the face of the immensity of His knowledge. Nay, immeasurable is the difference!'" No sooner had those words dropped from my lips than I found myself seized with fear and remorse, such as I could neither conceal nor explain. I bitterly reproved myself, and resolved at that very moment to alter my attitude and to soften my tone. I vowed to God that should my Host again refer to the subject, I would, with the utmost humility, answer and say: "If you be willing to substantiate your claim, you will most assuredly deliver me from the anxiety and suspense which so heavily oppress my soul. I shall truly be indebted to you for such deliverance." When I first started upon my quest, I determined to regard the two following standards as those whereby I could ascertain the truth of whosoever might claim to be the promised Qa'im. The first was a treatise which I had myself composed, bearing upon the abstruse and hidden teachings propounded by Shaykh Ahmad and Siyyid Kazim. Whoever seemed to me capable of unravelling the mysterious allusions made in that treatise, to him I would next submit my second request, and would ask him to reveal, without the least hesitation or reflection, a commentary on the Surih of Joseph, in a style and language entirely different from the prevailing standards of the time. I had previously requested Siyyid Kazim, in private, to write a commentary on that same Surih, which he refused, saying: "This is, verily, beyond me. He, that great One, who comes after me will, unasked, reveal it for you. That commentary will constitute one of the weightiest testimonies of His truth, and one of the clearest evidences of the loftiness of His position."

"'I was revolving these things in my mind, when my distinguished Host again remarked: "Observe attentively. Might not the Person intended by Siyyid Kazim be none other than I?" I thereupon felt impelled to present to Him a copy of the treatise which I had with me. "Will you," I asked Him, "read this book of mine and look at its pages with indulgent eyes? I pray you to overlook my weaknesses and failings." He graciously complied with my wish. He opened the book, glanced at certain passages, closed it, and began to address me. Within a few minutes He had, with characteristic vigour and charm, unravelled all its mysteries and resolved all its problems. Having to my entire satisfaction accomplished, within so short a time, the task I had expected Him to perform, He further expounded to me certain truths which could be found neither in the reported sayings of the imams of the Faith nor in the writings of Shaykh Ahmad and Siyyid Kazim. These truths, which I had never heard before, seemed to be endowed with refreshing vividness and power. "Had you not been My guest," He afterwards observed, "your position would indeed have been a grievous one. The all-encompassing grace of God has saved you. It is for God to test His servants, and not for His servants to judge Him in accordance with their deficient standards. Were I to fail to resolve your perplexities, could the Reality that shines within Me be regarded as powerless, or My knowledge be accused as faulty? Nay, by the righteousness of God! it behoves, in this day, the peoples and nations of both the East and the West to hasten to this threshold, and here seek to obtain the reviving grace of the Merciful. Whoso hesitates will indeed be in grievous loss. Do not the peoples of the earth testify that the fundamental purpose of their creation is the knowledge and adoration of God? It behoves them to arise, as earnestly and spontaneously as you have arisen, and to seek with determination and constancy their promised Beloved." He then proceeded to say: "Now is the time to reveal the commentary on the Súrih of Joseph." [30]

I have often asked myself and contemplated the idea of whether Mullá Husayn had a choice in recognizing the Báb. Although it seemed predestined, all of us have free will. Our free will distinguishes us from all of Creation. It is the essence of the dignity of man and provides the ladder upon which we ascend to the spiritual plane or descend to an existence lower than that of an animal.

Therefore Mullá Husayn had the free will to deny the Báb as well as to accept Him. If he had not exercised his will and recognized Him, we would never have heard of Mullá Husayn and someone else would have been the Bábu'l-Báb, the gate of the Gate. The story we would tell would be somewhat different, but perfect just as well. So, there is a lesson in the process as well as in the story.

The Báb gives us the first example of what a Fireside is and how it should be conducted. Let's examine what the Báb did. First, He met Mulla Husayn in the street and showered upon him love and kindness. He then invited this stranger to His home for refreshment and relaxation. Upon arriving at His home, Mulla Husayn was invited to wash up and the Báb served him refreshments personally. He engaged Mulla Husayn in conversation and invited him to tell of his travels and asked what he was seeking. After careful listening and creating an atmosphere that was safe and intimate, the Báb suggested that He might be the Object of Mulla Husayn's quest. Slowly yet determinedly, the Báb awoke Mulla Husayn to His Mission.

This was not a public event. It was a small gathering in one's home where intimacy was established and the guest felt safe to ask his most cherished questions. The host focused entirely on the seeker's needs and revealed only what was necessary to awaken first his curiosity and then his heart.

> It should not be overlooked, however, that the most powerful and effective teaching medium that has been found so far is the Fireside meeting, because in the Fireside meeting, intimate personal questions can be answered, and the student find the spirit of the Faith more abundant there.
>
> (From a letter dated 11 December 1952 written on behalf of Shoghi Effendi to a Local Spiritual Assembly and an individual believer) [31]

The Madness and the Method

How does this Fireside of the Báb contrast with the typical Fireside practices within the Bahá'i community? Many of the friends feel that they need a speaker; they need to invite as many people as possible; they must provide a formal atmosphere akin to a classroom; they must listen to a speaker and then finally provide some refreshment; and, if no seekers attend, it still counts to them as a Fireside because they did all the right stuff. Yet, nowhere in the Tablets or Talks of Ábdu'l Bahá or writings of Shoghi Effendi do they prescribe the Fireside in this manner. Nowhere do they suggest the frenetic pace of frantic teaching where the needs of and the sensitivity to the seeker are not viewed as paramount.

The Fireside is an activity that if done in accordance with the suggestions of Ábdu'l Bahá and Shoghi Effendi could transform society. Baha'u'llah suggests that teaching is something that we will be involved in throughout the duration of His Dispensation. "To assist Me is to teach My Cause. This is a theme with which whole Tablets are laden. This is the changeless commandment of God, eternal in the past, eternal in the future." [32]

Second, the idea of the Fireside gathering will also accompany us in that showing hospitality and developing strong friendships is at the center of community development. So, if teaching will be with us long after the entire world recognizes Baha'u'llah and the Fireside gathering will also be part of our lives, we must reexamine our understanding of the reality of the Fireside and its potential. We must not underestimate its value by viewing the Fireside as merely a mechanism to increase numbers.

Let's look at the attributes of the Fireside that Ábdu'l Bahá and Shoghi Effendi suggest. First of all, it takes place in one's home. That means that we must prepare our home for company. It probably means that we would attend to cleaning, preparing and making our home attractive. This doesn't mean expensive or ostentatious, but attractive to others. Some people are not used to having guests in their homes and will need to practice and learn. It means that we are willing to share our lives with someone else in an intimate way and learn to feel comfortable about it. It means that having someone visit us in our homes becomes a natural part of our lives, not an unusual event.

The Fireside process requires that we meet people other than members of our Bahá'i community and develop relationships with them that will encourage them to come to our homes. The process demands of us that we become so attractive to others that they will want to associate with us and visit us. It means that our personal activities be wider than just Bahá'i activities. Shoghi Effendi encourages us to become close friends with our neighbors and co-workers and possibly draw from that resource the potential new seekers. Of course, we must then act with extreme wisdom as we will continue to come into close contact with these neighbors and co-workers—probably for a long time and we will not want to alienate them by unwise action. The sensitivity of these contacts may be of particular and far-reaching importance when considering the complexities of the work environment and the increasing diversity of our neighborhoods.

Our evolving wisdom will determine how and when and under what circumstances we should bring up the Faith with our friends. It will require from us the judgment of whether our relationship with our friends provides an opportunity to speak of the Faith and in what context. It will cause us to rely on the Sacred Word and not solely on our own opinions, as we will want to bring the pure spring water to our contacts. We will probably want to have a few short passages memorized that can contribute to a conversation appropriately. And finally, we will be cautious not to over step the bounds of moderation in our discussions with our friends. Baha'u'llah, although enjoining us to teach, cautions us in *The Hidden Words*, "The wise are they that speak not unless they obtain a hearing…"[33]

So often our friends, neighbors and co-workers are wonderful people who do not demonstrate an interest in learning about the Bahá'í Faith or even inclined to spiritual ideas. However, if our friendships are close and there is trust, when our friends are startled and awakened through life's tests and trials or when the crumbling old order grabs them in an unkind way, they will seek our friendship and we may have an opportunity to respond with love and spiritual guidance.

I am reminded of the story of Queen Marie of Rumania and her interaction with the beloved Martha Root. Martha became her friend and during a time of intense personal test, Queen Marie was able to respond to

Martha on a spiritual plane and allowed the Message of Baha'u'llah to penetrate. In her own words, Queen Marie said, ""It came, as all great messages come, at an hour of dire grief and inner conflict and distress, so the seed sank deeply." [34]

The Fireside Process
==

The Fireside process as outlined by Shoghi Effendi involves six steps.

> The Baha'is must realize that the success of this work depends upon the individual. The individual must arise as never before to proclaim the Faith of Baha'u'llah. The most effective way for them to carry on their work is for the individual to make many contacts, select a few who they feel would become Baha'is, develop a close friendship with them, then complete confidence, and finally teach them the Faith, until they become strong supporters of the Cause of God.
> (Prom a letter dated 13 May 1955 written on behalf of Shoghi Effendi to all National Spiritual Assemblies) [35]

Step 1: Make many contacts
Step 2: Select a few who they feel would become Bahá'ís
Step 3: Develop a close friendship with them
Step 4: Complete confidence
Step 5: Finally teach them the Faith
Step 6: Until they become strong supporters of the Cause of God

The Fireside itself is an integral part of this process and takes place in one's home. It is intended to be an intimate gathering where hospitality is shown and people have an opportunity to have their questions answered in a safe setting.

> The Guardian hopes the Friends ... will display the loving spirit of the Master in their contacts, and then win those souls to the Faith. The fireside method of teaching seems to produce the greatest results, when each one invites friends into their homes once in nineteen days, and introduces them to the Faith. Close association and loving service affects the hearts; and when the heart is affected, then the spirit can enter. It is the Holy Spirit that quickens, and the Friends must become channels for its diffusion.
>
> (From a letter dated 27 January 1957 written on behalf of Shoghi Effendi to an individual believer)[36]

During the next chapters we will examine each of these steps and discover how we can put these steps into action.

5

Make Many Contacts

Consort with all men, O people of Bahá, in a spirit of friendliness and fellowship... A kindly tongue is the lodestone of the hearts of men. It is the bread of the spirit, it clotheth the words with meaning, it is the fountain of the light of wisdom and understanding... Gleanings from the Writings of Baha'u'llah, *p. 289*[37]

The Guardian tells us to make many contacts. How much is many? I know that a couple is two; that a few is probably somewhere between two and more than two—probably less than ten; several could be as few as six, but probably less than fifteen; and, many is more than a few and more than several. So, let's assume that many is more than fifteen. So, we need to make more than fifteen contacts.

For many of us (more than fifteen) our idea of how to make many contacts has been to go out and do something extraordinary like a teaching project, right? However, I would offer an alternative. It is probable that most of us come into contact with over fifteen people every week and some of us more than fifteen people every day—especially if we have a job outside of the home. And even for those of us who work in the home, we go shopping or to schools or somewhere where we have an opportunity to meet people. Making many contacts is part of our everyday life!

It's Even Scarier Out There Now

Not wanting to jump ahead, I would like to at least peek ahead to determine what to do while making many contacts. The Guardian tells that after making many contacts we are to determine who we believe could become Bahá'ís. Pretty powerful! We will not be able to know that unless we develop a relationship with our contacts over time and find out what they are interested in. We need to nurture our contacts into more than just saying "hello" at the cash register. We need to stand out from the rest of society in some way that is attractive to others.

We are not expected to be mystically anointed to look into someone's eyes and see if they are going to become a Bahá'í. And, we are not to be judgmental about someone's spiritual potential. We are, however, expected to develop relationships and determine if our relationship with someone can bear spiritual fruit. And that means extending friendship in meaningful ways. It means putting ourselves at risk by disclosing something about our personality while trying to interact. Not that a spiritual relationship should be a sole criteria for friendship. But, it should be the criteria if we are going to pursue or attempt to pursue teaching someone at the time. If not, then we can wait until the appropriate time arises in our friendships and then pursue teaching.

> Amanda has the ability to make many acquaintances and is like a butterfly with meeting people—touch a little here then go there and back and forth. Very quickly after

Amanda started at her new University, she had made many contacts across the campus. Amanda became friends with Maria almost as soon as she started at the University.

Maria was a very serious student who also loved the arts and performed a Latin folk dance. Amanda was a performing artist. Over the next year and a half, they saw each other occasionally and developed a friendship beyond just an acquaintance and when possible had a cup of coffee together or lunch.

The Bahá'í club on campus was really struggling and was in need of someone to lead the club who had good administrative skill. Amanda thought that Maria would be perfect except that Maria was not a Bahá'í. One day at lunch, Amanda was sharing her concern with Maria about the Bahá'í club. Not in a complaining way, but in a way that was sincere in that Amanda expressed her own shortcomings around administering the needs of the club.

Maria had heard of the Bahá'ís before and was curious. She asked if the club was open to everyone and could she participate. Amanda said of course and soon Maria was the President of the club. No better administrator could have been found. From the moment Maria became involved things started to happen that seemed to languish before. They were able to book rooms for events and things happened on time and more often.

Maria's boyfriend was working at a non-governmental organization that promotes the ideals of the United Nations. He had become attracted to the Bahá'í Faith over the years, but never pursued it. With Maria's activities at the University's Bahá'í club he became again interested and began to find out more about it in a formal way.

Amanda began inviting both Maria and her boyfriend over to her home where her parents could also meet them and begin to teach a little about the Faith. Soon the community began a very small Study Circle (about 6 people) and Amanda invited Maria and her boyfriend, Roger, to come if they wanted. They became very active participants and began visiting other Bahá'ís in the area and slowly became more and more attracted to the Teachings until they both enrolled.

Maria is now the Chairperson of her local Spiritual Assembly and she and Roger married after her graduation.

Amanda knew that becoming involved with people was the key to success as a teacher and would make her a happy person. Making many contacts in meaningful ways takes a little more time than our frantic lives sometime allow. But, if we are in tune with our purpose in life then we will build the discipline to try to make each encounter special.

Each time we meet someone we could identify that encounter as a potential opportunity for a new friend. We could see that person in a new light. We could be attracted to that person as a member of our family with eyes of recognition that they are part of our divine family.

> If thou wishest to guide the souls, it is incumbent on thee to be firm, to be good and to be inbued with praiseworthy attributes and divine qualities under all circumstances. Be a sign of love, a manifestation of mercy, a fountain of tenderness, kindhearted, good to all and gentle to the servants of God, and especially to those who bear relation to thee, both men and women. Bear every ordeal that befalleth thee from the people and confront them not save with kindness, with great love and good wishes.
>
> (*Tablets of Ábdu'l Bahá*, pp. 619-620) [38]

Who's Going to do the Community's Work

Many communities and especially Spiritual Assembly members are overwhelmed with community work. With the admonition to engage in the greater community to develop contacts that we may eventually be able to teach, the question of who will do the Bahá'i community work appears to be at odds. The Universal House of Justice has asked us to advance the process of entry by troops; our National Spiritual Assembly encourages us to build institutes and develop children's classes; the Auxiliary Board Members awaken us to our obligation to teach the Cause; and, the world around us gets more frenetic as the days go by. How do we compartmentalize all of this and still have time for our families and a little relaxation time to rejuvenate?

> A Texas Spiritual Assembly asked itself the same questions in its deliberations on how to plan for its small community of about 50 Bahá'is—adults, youth and children. It felt that although the community was a loving one, it fell short on its potential to serve the Faith and advance the process of entry by troops. In fact, it struggled with what advancement was and what did the House of Justice mean.

> As the Local Spiritual Assembly grappled with this problem, a concept began to emerge. The members began to understand that it was the idea of compartmentalization that was the problem. To try to compartmentalize our individual lives to serve all of the needs of the Faith was, in fact, a contributor to the dilemma. The real need was to integrate all of the needs, both the community's and the individual's needs, to advance the process of entry by troops.

> So, the Spiritual Assembly decided to hold a weekend planning session with the help of a

Facilitator and find out how to respond to the guidance from the House of Justice, the direction of the National Spiritual Assembly, the encouragement of the Auxiliary Board, the pace of today's society, and the individual needs of its community members into an integrated plan. They began to see that the process of entry by troops demanded integration and they wanted to find out how in their community they could advance it.

The LSA deliberations uncovered three major points: 1) the community needed to create a loving atmosphere, 2) they needed to enlarge the number of believers, and 3) the community needed to be more connected to the Creative Word on a routine basis.

They also realized that there were three primary tools at their disposal that would enable the success of their endeavors: 1) the Fund, 2) the Fireside, and 3) Study Circles. In their discussions, however, they turned to the Writings of the Faith and realized that neither of the three, with the exception perhaps to a small extent the Fund, was understood in terms of how the Center of the Faith described them. They began to discover that the manner in which Firesides were done was not in accordance with the guidance of 'Abdu'l-Bahá and Shoghi Effendi; that Study Circles as described in the House of Justice's 1995 letter were also misapplied; and, that even the Fund was not widely understood in terms of how monies were budgeted and spent.

The Spiritual Assembly created a strategic plan that was to be the center of all of their deliberations for the next two years. It would be the primary driver of the Assembly's agenda, the primary focus of consultation at Feast and, the spiritual motivator for each community member. Of course there would be other items that would emerge during that time, but they determined that all decisions of the Spiritual Assembly would be made within the context of the plan and that only with an extreme exception would they deviate from it. Unless, of course the plan needed to be modified as things changed. And then it would be done deliberately and not haphazardly. The plan was to become the central decision influencer for the Assembly.

First they came up with a two-year Vision for the community. (The text of their entire plan follows.) This was based on significant and soul-searching needs analysis followed by robust consultation. Upon completion of their Vision, they needed to determine how they could achieve it. In order to achieve their Vision they had to answer four fundamental questions about themselves and the community:

1. Are we doing what we are supposed to do?
2. Are we capable of doing what we should?
3. Are we using our resources effectively?
4. Do we administer the community efficiently?

They then began to identify four perspectives that required their attention. These were expansion, consolidation, process and, financial. The expansion perspective answered the question, "To ensure growth, how do we advance the process of entry by troops?" The consolidation perspective covered, "To achieve our Vision, how do we develop our Human Resources?" The financial perspective answered, "To achieve our Vision, how do we ensure financial health?" And finally, the process perspective considered, "To serve our community, how must we improve the way we administer?"

The Spiritual Assembly recognized that each of these perspectives were critical to the community's growth, but were also counter-balanced. Although all the perspectives affect one another, effort in one perspective naturally took effort that could not be applied in another. For example, an hour that one spends deepening cannot be spent balancing the Treasurer's budget or for every hour one holds a Fireside, he or she cannot use those hours to improve children's classes. So, the work of the community must be strategically focused for the most important tasks necessary to achieve the Vision. The Assembly also realized that the essence of strategy is sacrifice. We often must sacrifice the important for the most important.

The following describes the model that the Assembly used for the development of their plan followed by the plan itself. The plan has six primary areas with four of them described. For obvious reasons, we left off who and when. Based on realizing their Vision, they created Goals. From the Goals they identified Targets to achieve. The Targets were then committed to with Measures that ensured accomplishment. Lines of Action were identified for members of the community to become involved in that would contribute to the Goals. And finally, individuals were chosen to champion each Line of Action with Due Dates.

Now at Assembly meetings, the agenda first looks at progress in each Goal area with the Measures eventually providing data for potential decisions—reallocation of resources, identification of areas of concern for champions and reconsideration of Lines of Action to be accomplished. The plan also provides the Assembly's topics for consultation at Feasts in addition to other items brought up by the community.

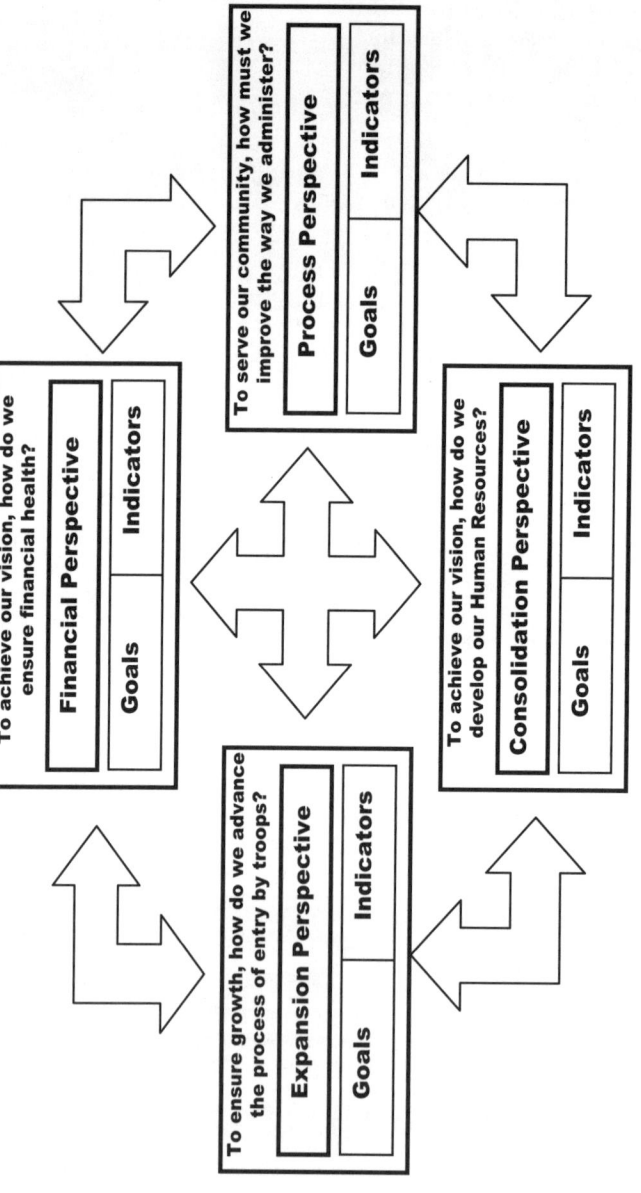

Figure 1

VISION: Develop a Nurturing, Attractive & Learning Environment that Fosters Intimate, Deepened Friendships

FINANCIAL PERSPECTIVE

GOALS	MEASURES	TARGETS	LINES OF ACTION		
			Project	Who	Due Date
• Improve the sustainability and consistency of the community's finances	IBP1. % participation in Fund IBP2. $ contributions per Baha'i month toward goal IBP3. % conformance w/NSA guidelines	IBP4. 70% participation in Fund per month IBP5. Conformance w/NSA financial guidelines by 2003 Audit	a. Educate community on financial needs and disbursements b. Educate community on auto-contributions and bill-pay c. Bring community finances into conformance w/NSA guidelines		

EXPANSION PERSPECTIVE

GOALS	MEASURES	TARGETS	LINES OF ACTION		
			Project	Who	Due Date
C2. Expand participation in Study Circles beyond the Baha'i community C3. Increase the number of personal firesides in the community	a. % LSA members with fireside buddy b. Total # firesides held	a. 10% of participants in Study Circles from beyond the Baha'i community b. 100% LSA members w/fireside buddy outside of LSA c. 150 firesides held within 18 months	a. Implement fireside teaching program b. Establish fireside monitoring process		

PROCESS PERSPECTIVE

GOALS	MEASURES	TARGETS	LINES OF ACTION		
			Project	Who	Due Date
a. Improve the process of establishing, mandating & monitoring committees b. Establish effective methods of communicating community information to all community members	a. Date of establishing, mandating & monitoring committees b. Time before event information communicated c. Community satisfaction survey	a. Establish committees by September 1st each year b. Establish committee monitoring system by September, 2003 c. Establish communication method by September, 2003	a. Establish process for community information updates b. Design effective communication methods c. Test, evaluate and implement new communication process		

CONSOLIDATION PERSPECTIVE

GOALS	MEASURES	TARGETS	LINES OF ACTION		
			Project	Who	Due Date
C1. Establish and expand Study Circle participation amongst all community members	F1. % participation of community members F2. # Study Circles on-going F3. # youth/child participants	a. 90% participation of community members in a Study Circle/year b. Minimum of 2 Study Circles on-going	a. Educate community on Study Circles b. LSA members facilitate Study Circle initiation c. Create community Study Circle Web site		

Figure 2

6
Select a Few

'Not everything that a man knoweth can be disclosed, nor can everything that he can disclose be regarded as timely, nor can every timely utterance be considered as suited to the capacity of those who hear it.' Such is the consummate wisdom to be observed in thy pursuits. Be not oblivious thereof, if thou wishest to be a man of action under all conditions. First diagnose the disease and identify the malady, then prescribe the remedy, for such is the perfect method of the skilful physician. Selections from the Writings of 'Abdu'l-Bahá, p. 269 [39]

To select a few who we believe can become Bahá'ís can be a daunting challenge. It appears that on the surface we are making a judgment as to whether this person has spiritual capacity or not. But, the selection process is not a judgment on one's spiritual capacity, rather it is a judgment on the level and condition of our relationship with that person.

We must judge whether our relationship with someone can bear spiritual fruit and when that fruit-bearing might take place. When 'Abdu'l-Bahá reminds us to consider not only the timeliness of our utterance, but the capacity of the situation, He is suggesting that with our words comes great responsibility. To say it another way from the Old Testament, "There is a time for every purpose under heaven." [40]

The Tuning Fork

Angela and her husband, Morris were devoted Christians who spent their lives seeking a community that practiced racial tolerance and diversity. Angela was a church-goer, but Morris was troubled with the racial separation within many Christian churches and kept his strong religious faith between God and himself and left the church out.

When they were in their early thirties, Morris was working in the national media and was involved in a story about a relatively unknown religion with a strange name, Bahá'í. He assisted in the publication of an article about the Faith and both he and Angela were attracted to the principles, especially about the oneness of mankind.

Soon after the article was published, Angela accelerated her study of the Faith and enrolled. However, Morris, although attracted, held back. Angela could not understand why and pushed Morris to study the Teachings and challenged him to remove his blinders. The more Angela wanted Morris to investigate, the more entrenched he became. So, she turned to prayer.

One night she stayed up very late wrapped in prayer continuously repeating a specific supplication to Baha'u'llah so that Morris would be drawn to becoming a Bahá'í. For hours she repeated a certain verse with tears running down her cheeks. Angela was a woman whose faith was very strong and her will equal to her faith. She knew that God would answer her prayers and bring Morris into the fold.

Suddenly, as Angela tells it, "I was struck by a Presence in the room and I became very quiet and afraid. Then a voice, quiet but commanding, said, 'Whose Faith do you think this is anyway?' I was chilled to the bone and I knew that I was in over my head. I realized that I needed to stop pestering Morris because his faith was between him and God and I was the problem."

Angela began to tune into the atmosphere that she created around herself in her approach to the Faith. She stopped discussing the Faith with Morris and concentrated on being a loving companion to him. In fact, she didn't mention the Faith at all. About a month later, Morris enrolled. Angela and Morris, now both professionally retired, have continued to serve the Faith with distinction in the United States, Haifa and internationally for over 40 years.

Angela learned a great lesson about the teaching process. She gained an insight into the boundaries we must honor when approaching so sacred an obligation. For Angela the lesson was visible and emphatic. For many of us the lessons are much harder and painful.

Many years ago, I made friends with a co-worker who was a very spiritually-oriented individual seeking fellowship from various religious communities. In my zeal to teach the Faith, I overstepped the bounds of moderation and spoke too forcefully about the fulfillment of the Prophecies of the world's religions in the Teachings of Baha'u'llah. I tried to awaken this pure-hearted seeker with arguments that proved the truth of my own faith and should have been apparent to any truth-seeker.

I will never forget the look of pain in that blessed person's eyes when I transgressed our friendship and the inoculation against the Bahá'í Faith was complete. Not only did I lose a friend, but I impaired a pure hearted soul's journey to God! I don't know if the inoculation was permanent, but I have prayed about that mistake many times over the years.

I think that that experience was a difficult gift for me. Many of us go through our teaching activities without reflecting on our actions and the repercussions of our behavior. For me, the experience is a constant reminder that we have been entrusted with a sacred gift that must be shared audaciously but with extreme wisdom. Shoghi Effendi has suggested that we must present the Faith as if we were bringing a gift to Royalty.

Beginning the Relationship

Relationships are about putting ourselves into a situation with another person with a degree of vulnerability. It requires disclosure. Not the kind of disclosure that brings discomfort to someone else, but the kind that builds trust and kinship. The more open we are with others the more they can open up to us. It is about connection in meaningful ways. Many of our relationships with co-workers and neighbors do not pass beyond the weather, sports, television and movies.

Learning how to ask penetrating, but kind and non-intrusive questions provides the key that can often unlock the potential for lasting friendships. Many people have similar wants, desires and experiences regardless of their ethnic origin or religious or racial background. Much of life's powerful influencers are common. Many of us have someone who cared for us in a special way, someone we admire or something that encourages and inspires us. Or, events that have brought to us pain and anguish or provoke anger. This provides great opportunity for learning about each other.

For many of us it is difficult going beyond superficial conversation to find out who we are under the surface. Yet, it is the deeper level of connection that many people hunger for whether they are conscious of it or not. Over the years, I have used an intimacy exercise in many of the workshops I have facilitated that stimulates a more meaningful conversation between people. We call it the Intimacy Exercise and I include it below. The questions can be a great source of friendship-building and are often a revelation to people who have been very close friends for years.

The Intimacy Exercise[41]

In a conversation, take turns asking your partner a question. Continue taking turns. Choose those that interest you the most, following the rules below:

Anything said must be held in confidence.
You do not have to answer every question your partner asks.
Do not ask your partner a question unless you are willing to answer the same one.

1. Who is or was the most influential person in your life?
2. Who is the most important person in your life?
3. As a child, what did you want to be when you grew up?
4. What qualities do you look for in a friend?
5. What was the most "successful" experience you've ever had?
6. How do you have fun?
7. Describe your parents.
8. Who is your best friend?
9. Has anyone ever betrayed your trust? How?
10. If you could be anything you wanted, what would it be?
11. What do you value most?
12. Where would you really like to live?
13. What do you want to be doing 10 years from now?
14. What makes you angry or annoyed?
15. What is difficult for you?

16. What kind of people do you like best?
17. What was your most embarrassing moment?
18. What do you want people to say about you after you've died?
19. Do you usually show your feelings or hide them?
20. Describe yourself in 5 words or less.
21. What is your best personal quality?
22. What is your worst habit?
23. Is money an important goal for you?
24. Describe a unique communication problem you have had.
25. What is your favorite music?
26. Are you a leader or a follower?
27. In what ways do you want to be like your parents?
28. How do you want your children to be like you?
29. How do you want your children to be different than you?
30. What fascinates you?
31. What bores you?
32. Describe your ideal life
33. Where would like to travel?
34. What do you think of me?
35. Do you like yourself?
36. Who do you want to like you?
37. Is there anyone else you'd rather be?
38. What do you most regret not doing?
39. What are you most proud of doing?
40. If you could transform any other person, who would it be and in what way?

7
Develop a Close Friendship

The friends of God should weave bonds of fellowship with others and show absolute love and affection towards them. These links have a deep influence on people and they will listen. When the friends sense receptivity to the Word of God, they should deliver the Message with wisdom. They must first try and remove any apprehensions in the people they teach. In fact, every one of the believers should choose one person every year and try to establish ties of friendship with him, so that all his fear would disappear. Only then, and gradually, must he teach that person. This is the best method. 'Abdu'l-Baha, in The Individual and Teaching: Raising the Divine Call, p. 12[42]

For many of us, we go through life with very few truly close friends with whom we have bonds of fellowship that penetrate deep into our lives. These relationships are often more cherished than even our family relationships. What a great bounty it would be if we could expand our friendship arena and create relationships like this with many people.

Imagine if every year we increased our circle of very close friends by one. Over the course of a lifetime, we would be at the center of a loving blanket that would hold us aloft through any test or trial. And if, we were only partially successful in teaching those friends, the circle of new Bahá'ís would increase dramatically.

This Takes Work

In the 1980's there was a campaign in the United States instigated by the Hand of the Cause, William Sears in response to an injunction of 'Abdu'l-Baha entitled, *Each One Teach One*. There was even a song written with the same name and sung at many of the Bahá'i Schools.

> Jeremy went to Green Acre Bahá'i School as a child and youth and remembers well the song, *Each One Teach One*. It penetrated deep into his heart and he believed that it was directed to him personally. He has a radiance of spirit about him and although he is a shy person, he makes friends easily.
>
> In 10th grade, Jeremy's family moved into a new school district and he had to develop a whole new crop of friends. Jeremy and Mark hit it off almost immediately. They both joined the school's drama club and were in several school plays together. They were inseparable.
>
> Mark's family was a wonderful and loving family and they were very kind to Jeremy as well as Jeremy's family to Mark. Mark's family did not believe in God and never taught him about spiritual things. They did teach Mark that he had a responsibility to society and had to give community service as part of his role in life. Jeremy's family was peculiar to Mark in that they spoke freely of God and one's relationship to a spiritual journey.

Over the course of a couple of years, Mark began to become attracted to the Teachings that animated Jeremy's life. Jeremy was very careful not to overwhelm Mark and shared the Teachings only on request and even then very slowly. When Mark suggested in his senior year of high school that he wanted to learn more about the Faith in a formal way, Jeremy wanted to share something with Mark's parents so they would not be worried.

Jeremy asked his parents if he could invite Mark's parents over to the house to explain to them the Teachings of the Faith. Not to teach them, but to help them understand that the Faith was an acceptable path for Mark to pursue. So, they arranged a dinner and Mark's parents came to visit.

The evening was delightful and the conversation was casual. Mark's parents were a little uncomfortable speaking about religion as they did not want to be preached to and they weren't interested in joining anything. Jeremy and his parents spoke in a loving manner without any pressure or expectation. In fact, they mentioned that the only reason they wanted to have Mark's parents know anything was so that they would not be concerned for Mark if he chose to pursue becoming a Bahá'í. The evening was a great success and both families have remained friends for many years.

A few months later Mark became a Bahá'í with his parents' blessings. A couple of years later during his college years, Jeremy met a young woman and married. Mark was his best man. A few years after that Mark met a young woman and married. Jeremy was his best man. Although they have moved away from each other due to careers, they still speak weekly; share their experiences about careers and serving on their respective Spiritual Assemblies; and, complain and rejoice about the difficulties of growing older and raising families and careers in a crazy world.

For Jeremy, making good friends is the object of life. The fact that this good friend also became a Bahá'í was *icing on the cake*. Other friends who have not become Bahá'is are still close because Jeremy understands that making strong friendships brings joy to him and fulfills his spiritual obligation to edify the souls of others. Edify means to raise up someone's faith and Jeremy's friends, whether they are Bahá'í or not, have faith in their friendship with Jeremy and also know that he is a Bahá'í just as they know that he loves soccer, video games and a good hamburger.

Can I Develop This Much Happiness

When 'Abdu'l-Baha enjoins upon us to live the Bahá'í life it seems obvious that He means to live a spiritual life according to the Teachings of the Faith. I have often contemplated not only what it meant to me philosophically, but how might I apply it in my daily affairs. Living the Bahá'í life certainly infers that we do many things differently than the generality of society.

However, it also suggests that we do that which others also do in a spiritualized fashion.

For example, when we make friends, we see those friendships as a spiritual engagement that has the potential to last beyond this lifetime. We make friends for the sake of God and not for the sake of our own benefit, even though we gain much through having friends. Our vested interest is to please God by serving humanity and bringing healing spiritual food to our daily activities and encounters.

'Abdu'l-Baha commands us to "Be happy!" These are not just the words of a kindly old man. These are a commandment of God. We have a spiritual obligation to be happy. Baha'u'llah has instructed us that, *man should know his own self and recognize that which leadeth unto loftiness or lowliness, glory or abasement, wealth or poverty* .[43] Living a full, rich life and developing long lasting and deep friendships provides a wealth that we can draw upon through tests and trials and during times of ease and fulfillment.

> There are four kinds of love. The first is the love that flows from God to man...The second is the love that flows from man to God. This is faith...The third is the love of God towards the Self or Identity of God...Through one ray of this Love all other love exists...The fourth is the love of man for man. The love which exists between the hearts of believers is prompted by the ideal of the unity of spirits. This love is attained through the knowledge of God, so that men see the Divine Love reflected in the heart. Each sees in the other

the Beauty of God reflected in the soul, and finding this point of similarity, they are attracted to one another in love. This love will make all men the waves of one sea, this love will make them all the stars of one heaven and the fruits of one tree. This love will bring the realization of true accord, the foundation of real unity. ('Abdu'l-Baha, *Paris Talks*, p. 181)[44]

Our true happiness comes from our belief in God and obedience to His Covenant. Through this belief and obedience our ability to become attractive to others and develop deep friendships is enhanced. We begin to connect to others in ways that we couldn't imagine and God uses us to further His Purpose. We gain by being allowed to play a part in God's great Drama and we become increasingly more happy. *"Even or odd, thou shalt win the wager." The friends of God shall win and profit under all conditions, and shall attain true wealth. In fire they remain cold, and from water they emerge dry. Their affairs are at variance with the affairs of men. Gain is their lot, whatever the deal. To this testifieth every wise one with a discerning eye, and every fair-minded one with a hearing ear.* (Baha'u'llah, *Crises and Victory*, p. 155)[45]

Now I am Really Scared!

Making friends for many of us is somewhat easy. For others it is difficult. However, whether making friends is easy or difficult, moving from casual friendships to deep ones can be very scary. It means letting someone inside to see our vulnerabilities. It means putting our guard down a bit. Deep friendships, those that penetrate our lives for a long time, require disclosure. Not the kind of disclosure that borders on confession, but the kind that brings our hearts together. We share our worries, our fears, our joys, sometimes our failures and our victories.

Moving from casual friendship to deep friendship is risky, delicate and time-consuming. In order to develop deep friendships we must simply put in the time. And in this day and age, for many of us, time is our most cherished commodity—once spent, it cannot be recovered.

> John was transferred to corporate headquarters after several distinguished field assignments. He was to become a facilitator for training new recruits to the corporation. This was a prestigious assignment and one that would stretch his talents, develop new ones and serve as a launching pad to executive development. The training he was to go through lasted for two months. There were about 10 others going through the process at the same time from several business units throughout the corporation.
>
> Donna participated during the first weeks of the program. She was a visiting lecturer from a local University and both participated and lectured. On the second day of her participation, she was paired up with John in an experiential exercise. During the debriefing of the exercise, she noticed John's Bahá'í ring and asked what it was and did it have any significance.

John casually mentioned that it was his Bahá'í ring and that the symbols had spiritual significance and he returned his attention to the class leader. Donna's curiosity, however, went into high gear. She wanted to know what was the spiritual significance and what was that word that he said that started with a "B".

At the end of the day, as everyone was filing out to go home, Donna cornered John and asked him again about his ring. John tried to beg off the discussion, but Donna pleasantly insisted. So, John said, "Do you really want to know?" Of course this just charged her curiosity more.

John sat down for a few minutes and explained very briefly the symbolism of his ringstone and that it was a sacred word from his Faith that meant "O thou Glory of the All-Glorious." Donna asked that he tell her a little about his Faith. So, John spoke very briefly about the central tenets of the Faith, describing that Bahá'is believe that there is only one God, that He manifests Himself periodically throughout history to mankind, that all religions emanate from the same Source, and that all of humankind is part of one family. Donna wanted to know more.

John suggested that they have a conversation at another time away from work if she still had an interest. Over the course of the next several months, John and his wife, MaryLynn, invited Donna to their home many times and slowly discussed different aspects of the Faith. They became very attracted to one another and their personal friendships grew. Donna came to visit at least weekly for dinner, desert, coffee, just to say "hello", or to ask another question that was stirred by a previous conversation.

Slowly, Donna became a part of their family. During these months, John and MaryLynn began to introduce Donna to other handpicked members of the Bahá'í community who they thought could also become friends with her. As Donna's study of the Writings and Teachings of the Faith intensified, her desire to meet more and more of the community also increased. John and MaryLynn were very concerned that her understanding of the Central Figures of the Faith be sufficient before they expanded her exposure to the general Bahá'í community.

At the suggestion of one of the other Bahá'í couples that Donna had become close with, they planned a gathering at their home where a larger group of local Bahá'ís could attend. But, in an atmosphere where they could still maintain some control if anyone became too zealous in discussion. The evening was a success. They continued to hold small gatherings in their home weekly and Donna became a regular.

Slowly, after about a year and a half, Donna enrolled in the Faith. Her deepening process began with her friendship with John and MaryLynn and continues. Donna developed a passion for teaching. Several years later, after John and MaryLynn moved to a different part of the country, Donna went on a vacation cruise.

While on the cruise she got into a conversation with one of the other couples and the topic of peculiar last names came up. Donna mentioned that she had some friends who had a peculiar last name and when she said what it was, the couple on the cruise said, "And I bet their first names must be John and MaryLynn!" Donna was amazed. The couple was John and MaryLynn's next-door neighbors! Donna was thrilled that she could say why John and MaryLynn were friends and it opened the door for a conversation about the Faith. And the couple were thrilled when they got back to share the experience with their neighbors.

John and MaryLynn invested a lot of time in developing their friendship with Donna. They are still good friends today. The reward was great, but the time it took was great too. With our lives as hectic as they are, it requires from us a discipline and focus that too often is too easy to dismiss.

We cannot imagine how our lives interconnect with others beyond the obvious. Donna made a contact with another couple across the ocean that connected to her good friends and their neighbors. The seeds that we sow travel to unexpected corners and only God can unlock the mysterious power latent within them.

The Guardian enjoins upon us to make *the mandate of teaching, so vitally binding upon all, the all-pervading concern of his life.* [46] This mandate empowers us to develop the discipline and focus and relieves us of the fear of failure.

> In his daily activities and contacts, in all his journeys, whether for business or otherwise, on his holidays and outings, and on any mission he may be called upon to undertake, every bearer of the Message of Baha'u'llah should consider it not only an obligation but a privilege to scatter far and wide the seeds of His Faith, and to rest content in the abiding knowledge that whatever be the immediate response to that Message, and however inadequate the vehicle that conveyed it, the power of its Author will, as He sees fit, enable those seeds to germinate, and in circumstances which no one can foresee enrich the harvest which the labor of His followers will gather.
>
> Shoghi Effendi, *Advent of Divine Justice,* p. 53[47]

Scattering far and wide the seeds of our Faith does not mean without wisdom. I think that the Guardian is suggesting that we scatter far and wide our friendships and be not overly concerned with whether someone becomes a Bahá'í or not. The attraction of one's soul to the Message of Baha'u'llah remains an intimate intercourse between an individual and his or her Creator. The germination of those seeds depends on the power of that intercourse and not on the efficacy of our friendships. However, the limitations of our friendships could hinder that greater harvest.

8
Complete Confidence

Finally, we come to the kingdom of man. As this is the superior kingdom, the light of love is more resplendent. In man we find the power of attraction among the elements which compose his material body, plus the attraction which produces cellular admixture or augmentative power, plus the attraction which characterizes the sensibilities of the animal kingdom, but still beyond and above all these lower powers we discover in the being of man the attraction of heart, the susceptibilities and affinities which bind men together, enabling them to live and associate in friendship and solidarity. It is, therefore, evident that in the world of humanity the greatest king and sovereign is love. If love were extinguished, the power of attraction dispelled, the affinity of human hearts destroyed, the phenomena of human life would disappear. ('Abdu'l-Baha, Promulgation of Universal Peace, p. 256)[48]

Imagine when the development of the power of love is unleashed throughout the world. How the power of attraction would bind the peoples of the world in such a way that no potential of disputes or war could penetrate! The attainment of such a world depends on the ability of the individual to forge friendships beyond our historic experience.

> The most effective way for them to carry on their work is for the individual to make many contacts, select a few who they feel would

become Baha'is, develop a close friendship with them, then complete confidence, and finally teach them the Faith, until they become strong supporters of the Cause of God.(Shoghi Effendi)[49]

What does the Guardian mean when says after we have developed close friendships we should *complete confidence*? It is interesting to point out that "complete" in this sentence, is used as a verb and not an adjective or an adverb. He does not say "with complete confidence". The action "to complete" suggests that beyond close friendship there is another stage in the development of the relationship. When we think of the close friendships we have with others, with how many of them have we completed confidence and what is the difference in those relationships?

With a marriage partner, we would complete confidence in that the trust between spouses, in a mature marriage, would be extremely high. We would trust each other with our very lives. We would certainly trust each other with the care and safety of our children and our finances. There would only be a thin veil between us that we *would overstep not*[50] as 'Abdu'l-Baha suggests in a prayer for marriage. The friendships between family members oftentimes are akin to the relationships of marriage.

So what of relationships outside of marriage and family? Are there similarities or comparisons to be made in those relationships as well? When we have that kind of relationship, our deepest thoughts and sincerest beliefs can be shared in complete trust. We would not be insecure in sharing our thoughts and feelings and our friends would not think less of us or become wary of us for having our thoughts and feelings.

The beloved Guardian suggests that we must reach this stage <u>before</u> we teach the Cause. How different an approach from the way we currently engage in teaching!

<u>How long will it take?</u>

Developing our relationships takes time. The time from acquaintance to close friendship to confidence cannot be measured in time. It must be measured by its quality and nature. For many of us, our close friendships have not been tempered by the fire of tests, so we cannot judge the hardness of their steel or bond.

Often we find out about the quality of our relationships during times of severe tests. We may go through a severe test and find out who supports us and who assists us unasked. We have a disagreement on a point and find out how strong our bond can withstand the tension. At other times we find that we are not sensitive to another's condition and learn how little we really know of them. With others, we are super-sensitive to their situation and come to their aid at a critical time.

> Mary and Helen were very close friends for a long time. Some time after Mary had become a Bahá'í, she gave Helen a book about the Faith. Helen was a strong Catholic and very devoted. Helen gave her, *Some Answered Questions* by 'Abdu'l-Bahá as a gift.

Helen thanked her for the book, but didn't mention it again. Several years later, Mary married and moved to another country. Years passed and they lost touch with each other.

A few years more passed and Helen went through a severe crisis in her life. During her moments of grief and distress, Mary came into her mind and she longed for that loving friend. She remembered that Mary had given her a book and she decided to find it and read it.

She couldn't remember what it was about, but she wanted to read it to feel close to Mary and knew that it must be special. Helen dug through her things until she found that book that she had saved all these years.

Helen was excited through her reading and realized that she must contact the Bahá'ís. She began attending small gatherings in some of the believers' homes and earnestly began studying about the Teachings. One of the Bahá'ís mentioned that she was in touch with Mary and after all the years they re-connected both in mind and spirit.

Had Mary not developed such a loving and trusting friendship with Helen, Helen would not have cherished the book she was given. Through friendship, Helen was able to trust the words in the book and pursue the Bahá'i community. Though many years had passed, the efficacy of their relationship withstood the test of time and place.

How will I know?

Knowing when we have completed confidence with someone reminds me of the question, how do you know you are in love? There is no checklist or defined criteria. The completion of confidence in our relationships evolves. We test our relationships along the development path and become more and more secure in them as they grow and mature. Unfortunately, we have no meter that rings when our relationships mature. However, I think that there is an internal bell that goes off as we approach the level of trust we require to feel confidence in our relationships and that signals our ability to accelerate our trust.

Sometimes a precipitous event helps to accelerate the development of our friendships. Often during times of significant crisis, the timeframe that usually occurs for friendships to develop is compressed. There are numerous stories of how people have endured life-threatening situations with others that create deep and enduring, lifelong friendships.

> Isabel and her family immigrated to the United States from the Caribbean and purchased a home in the part of the city that encouraged inter-racial and diverse peoples to live. The neighbors next door were an interesting family who had adopted multi-racial children and had many visitors to their home on a weekly basis.
>
> The family members would say hello as they passed Isabel and often over the fence between the yards they would stand and carry

on a small conversation. The families were courteous with one another, but kept a comfortable distance. Isabel was curious about this different family, but was not inclined to ask very many questions as is common especially among immigrant families.

In the neighborhood, there was an incident that precipitated considerable dialogue about racial issues and the tension was high. This gave rise to an opportunity for Isabel and her neighbors to talk more frequently and in a more meaningful manner than previously.

Sharon and Mark were very different than most Americans that Isabel had met. They were very upfront with their concerns for racial harmony and developing community relations. In fact, Mark was passionate and angry when he spoke about the injustices that he saw in the dialogue about the incident in the neighborhood. Mark was a white man angry with the treatment of African-Americans in his neighborhood. How peculiar!

Slowly, Isabel lowered her guard with these different and kind neighbors. She accepted an invitation to visit in Sharon's home. This was the first time she visited in an American's home who was not from Caribbean descent. Although the first few minutes were awkward, the friendliness and true spirit of fellowship overwhelmed her. She liked this family.

Isabel's husband was much more reserved than Isabel, but he too was taken with the courtesy and kindness of his neighbors. The children of both families became friends and started to visit each other's homes. Over time the friendship between the families grew into one of great respect and trust. As the community around them continued to become embroiled in the current situation, these families were a beacon of hope for cross-racial relations.

They hung onto each other during the crises and shored up each other's confidence to weather the storm. Of course, things in the neighborhood calmed down and an air of safety and harmony again covered the area. It was a great and unique neighborhood with people dedicated to demonstrating the possibility of the races living in harmony. Most people who lived in the neighborhood moved there for the diversity and even during times of difficulties would not think of leaving.

Sharon and Mark consulted often about the possibility of teaching Isabel about the Bahá'í Faith. Although Mark was an enthusiastic teacher, both he and Sharon determined to go slowly and cautiously with introducing the Faith to Isabel.

Isabel, on the other hand, wanted to know why Sharon and Mark were so dedicated to racial harmony and what animated their lives. But, she was reluctant to ask as she did not want to affect the friendship that was developing with too personal a question.

Over time, Sharon and Mark would casually mention that they were going to this or that event and were Bahá'ís. Eventually, there was an event at their home that they felt they could invite Isabel to where it would be safe. This began an intense and long study for Isabel that led to her acknowledging her belief in Baha'u'llah. Her children also became interested and became Bahá'ís. Although her husband has not yet become a Bahá'i, he goes to all of the events and helps out more than many of the Bahá'ís. He is loved and cherished by the community and enjoys being with the community whenever possible.

Isabel and her family were a gift to Sharon and Mark and the entire Bahá'i community. The relationship that was developed between the families and the confirmations that their friendship brought to Sharon and Mark reflect the abiding efficacy in following the guidance given by the Guardian on how to teach the Faith.

9
Finally Teach the Faith

He fully realizes that the demands made upon the Baha'is are great, and that they often feel inadequate, tired and perhaps frightened in the face of the tasks that confront them. This is only natural. On the other hand, they must realize that the power of God can and will assist them; and that because they are privileged to have accepted the Manifestation of God for this Day, this very act has placed upon them a great moral responsibility toward their fellow men. It is this moral responsibility to which the Guardian is constantly calling their attention. . . . Written on behalf of Shoghi Effendi, in *The Individual and Teaching: Raising the Divine Call*, p. 37[51]

Throughout this book, many of the stories have resulted in people becoming Bahá'ís. In each case it was at the end of a loving process that built on friendships that were developed and nurtured. Teaching the Faith should be a natural outgrowth of sharing one's life with another. When we become friends with someone who is Jewish it is natural that they will speak of their life as a practicing Jew. When we are friends with a Christian, it is natural that they will speak of activities of their church. The same will occur with anyone from any religion or belief system that we would exchange information about our life's activities.

And in that sharing process, if someone shows an interest in part of our lives, we would talk about it. Not with the intent of conversion, but in the desire to share our life with them. The Bahá'í life is one of service to the Cause—and service to the Cause is teaching His Message. But we teach first and foremost by our life's example that hopefully will attract others to seek out our way of life.

If we firmly believe that Baha'u'llah has come to bring the healing Message of God for this day, then it is only natural that we should have the passion to share with others this news. But it must be done with love, wisdom and for the sake of God and the sake of the seeker.

The Risk and the Reward

Many years ago I was privileged to be an Auxiliary Board Assistant to Mrs. Javidukht Khadem. It was one of the great experiences of my life. Once when we were in a training session on how to be an Assistant, Mrs. Khadem said, "It not as important to love the friends as it is to let them love you."

That statement was life-changing for me. It sent a shock through my system. It re-oriented my perspective on relationships. What she was saying was that loving someone else is easy if you use your own criteria on what loving is. But if you are concentrating on letting them love you, you must center your attention on them and their needs. You must become attractive to them in order to let them love you. It puts one in a service mode by serving their need for love and not serving your personal need to express love. This is the essence of the process of teaching.

Imagine trying to teach someone something they did not want to learn or something that they already knew. They would not be interested in knowing. But if it was something that they wanted to learn, you would have their full attention. My daughter didn't have nearly as much interest in learning how to add and subtract as she did when it involved her allowance and her chores. There really is *a time for every purpose under heaven.*

> Ginger and Rob were very active seekers attending numerous Bahá'í teaching meetings. Right up to the moment they were married, they went to meetings every week. About two weeks before the marriage, Ginger decided to become a Bahá'í. Rob said he wasn't quite ready and held back. So Ginger enrolled and was immediately embraced by the small Bahá'í community in their area.
>
> Shortly following their marriage, Rob announced that there would be no more of that Bahá'í stuff and forbid any mention of it and made it extremely hard for Ginger to participate in anything. If she suggested that she wanted to go to a meeting or call one of the Bahá'ís it would cause a big argument.
>
> Ginger knew that there were two sacred principles in her newly adopted Faith. One was the striving for unity in general and the other was the sanctity and unity of marriage. So, Ginger decided that she would forego any

Bahá'í activities, say her prayers and read the Bahá'í Writings in private, and be as supportive to her husband as possible.

Over the next five years they had three children and Ginger enthusiastically participated in Rob's church life with him. She never complained about her loss of the Bahá'í community and was involved in the church activities without herself becoming a formal member.

One night Rob expressed that he was becoming again disillusioned with his church, just as he had been when they were first investigating the Bahá'í Teachings. Ginger just nodded, said nothing and listened to his complaints.

A few weeks later, Rob stopped participating and going to church. Ginger tried to be as supportive as she could. A short while later, Rob said that he thought that maybe they should again try the Bahá'ís. They attended a Bahá'í Fireside in the home of one of the local Bahá'ís. That evening Rob enrolled!

When I met them a year or so later, they were at the center of the largest teaching event of the area where, almost solely from the work of Rob and Ginger, over sixty people had enrolled in the Faith. Rob became involved in a migrant worker program assisting the migrant workers and their families with school and housing. From that work he slowly began inviting the new friends he was making to his home where they held study meetings on the Bahá'í Writings.

After the interest began expanding, they began to hold the study classes at the migrant camps and people started to enroll by the tens. Many of the new Bahá'ís were only there during the fruit-picking season and then went back home to their native countries where they contacted the local Bahá'ís in their home communities.

Ginger's patience, long-suffering and dedication to the principles of the Faith brought her gifts beyond her imagination. If not for her steadfastness in her Faith and in her marriage, she not only may have lost a wonderful companion, but her husband may not have found his Faith.

Life is hard and maintaining relationships, when our entire society has about as much patience as a 30-minute soap opera, is almost impossible. But the rewards are great and the spiritual benefits incalculable.

Teaching is a process—a patient, tactful and determined process.

10

Until They Become Strong

True consolidation is to ensure that the love of Baha'u'llah and devotion to His Faith are firmly rooted in the hearts of the believers; this is the essential foundation for the subsequent addition of increased knowledge of the teachings and the development of the Bahá'í way of life.
Letter from the Universal House of Justice, dated November 3, 1974, to a National Spiritual Assembly, in an unpublished compilation prepared by the International Teaching Center[52]

To give people this glorious Message and then leave them in the lurch, produces disappointment and disillusionment, so that, when it does become possible to carry out properly planned teaching in that area, the teachers may well find the people resistant to the Message. The first teacher who was careless of consolidation, instead of planting and nourishing the seeds of faith has, in fact "inoculated" the people against the Divine Message and made subsequent teaching very much harder.
Letter written on behalf of the Universal House of Justice, dated April 16, 1981, to all Continental Pioneer Committees[53]

In many areas where large numbers of people have enrolled in the Faith, the difficulties with consolidation last for many years. This is not to condemn in any way the blessing of new believers who in most cases are sincere seekers and converts to the Teachings of Baha'u'llah. Nor is it meant to be critical of the stalwart teachers of the Faith. However, to me it underscores the benefits of developing strong friendships prior to teaching the Cause. If we have developed strong friendships, the process of consolidation becomes a continuation of our relationships.

Today, in addition to the friendships that we build, we have several successful tools at our disposal. The House of Justice's encouragement to the friends to establish Study Circles at the grass roots provides a powerful consolidation tool. Our increasingly developed local schools and institutes offer places to deepen new enrollments and their families and involve the community in the process of friendship-building.

The Coach

Baha'u'llah, 'Abdu'l-Baha and Shoghi Effendi suggest that the relationship between teacher and seeker is one of spiritual parent and spiritual child. Like the care and nurturing of a loving parent in the development of the child, the spiritual teacher shoulders a responsibility of care and nurturing for the spiritual child. This means assisting with his or her Bahá'í education and with his or her involvement in the community.

> Let him not be content until he has infused into his spiritual child so deep a longing as to impel him to arise independently, in his turn, and devote his energies to the quickening of other souls, and the upholding of the laws and principles laid down by his newly adopted Faith.
> Shoghi Effendi, *The Advent of Divine Justice*, p. 52[54]

From the beginning of the seeker's interest in the Faith through to the moment of enrollment, the teacher's responsibility to nurture, encourage and coach is apparent. A coach's job is to provide feedback, potential direction to pursue, encouragement and critical support during one's development. Even those whose talent and potential far exceeds that of the coach need the loving guidance and feedback. In fact, oftentimes the coach's talent is dwarfed by the talent of those to whom he or she provides coaching.

Luciano Pavarotti, one of the great opera tenors of our time, has a coach to assist him. He needs a competent and caring eye to watch him and provide suggestions on how to grow and develop. Performers, Athletes and Executives in corporations all use coaches to improve their performance.

The new believer also requires close, loving guidance during the tender process of becoming an active and contributing community member. Even our communities use a coach. One of the roles that the Institution of the Auxiliary Board provides is coaching for the local Spiritual Assemblies and individual Bahá'is in their desire to fulfill the plans of the Faith's Institutions. For the new believer, the best coach is his or her teacher with whom he or she has already developed a loving and close friendship.

The recent development of Study Circles and Institutes provide not only an assistance to the individual becoming a Bahá'i, but also gives the teacher another avenue for the development of their personal teaching process and fostering friendships. The transition from Fireside teaching to a combination of the Fireside and a

Study Circle or small Institute class, as the seeker's interest increases, may offer a more careful and protected environment to introduce a seeker to other believers.

A Study Circle based on common interests or on a more formal Ruhi process brings a new seeker or believer into direct contact with the Creative Word to further enhance his or her deepening in a newly awakened belief.

> Where a training institute is well established and constantly functioning, three core activities--study circles, devotional meetings, and children's classes--have multiplied with relative ease. Indeed, the participation of seekers in these activities, at the invitation of their Baha'i friends, has lent a new dimension to their purposes, consequently effecting new enrolments. Here, surely, is a direction of great promise for the teaching work. These core activities, which at the outset were devised principally to benefit the believers themselves, are naturally becoming portals for entry by troops. By combining study circles, devotional meetings and children's classes within the framework of clusters, a model of coherence in lines of action has been put in place and is already producing welcome results. Worldwide application of this model, we feel confident, holds immense possibilities for the progress of the Cause in the years ahead.
> Universal House of Justice, Ridvan, 159

The Community

For some, the consolidation process, the process that brings new believers into strong participation in the work of the Faith, takes a very short period of time. For others, the development of new patterns of behavior can take a long time. In either case, the Guardian puts tremendous responsibility on the individual teacher and the community to assist in this process.

> Morgan enrolled in the Faith as a young man in his twenties and immediately began to involve himself in the teaching work of the Faith. However, hidden from his teaching activities and the view of his newly adopted community, Morgan struggled with the scourge of alcoholism. Over the years, Morgan married, was occasionally appointed to serve on various community and area committees and to outward appearances displayed an exemplary Bahá'í life.

> Morgan and his wife, Shirley, had children and made sure that the children were involved in Bahá'í activities and Bahá'í schools. Over time, Morgan's alcoholism became an increasing problem and Shirley went to the local Spiritual Assembly for assistance. The local Spiritual Assembly encouraged Morgan to get professional help and he complied intermittently over the next couple of years. But, Morgan just didn't have the will or the discipline to stop his drinking. His behavior became increasingly problematic for his family and the community.

Finally, the Spiritual Assembly felt that its assistance was having no effect and Morgan's behavior began to create in public, a problem. They felt that administrative sanctions needed to be applied. The Assembly sought to curb Morgan's ability to serve in any administrative capacity where his behavior would reflect poorly on the Bahá'í community and its institutions. So, the Spiritual Assembly recommended to the National Spiritual Assembly that Morgan's administrative rights be removed.

The loss of his administrative rights was a severe blow to Morgan. He fell into a depressive state and deeply admonished himself for his lack of courage and discipline to curb his alcoholism. He finally realized the depths of his spiritual state and began to seriously deal with his problem. Morgan got himself professional help and began to attend Alcoholics Anonymous meetings regularly. After a few short months, Morgan was completely dry.

Morgan stopped drinking for many months and returned to the Spiritual Assembly with his limited victory and asked for reinstatement of his administrative rights. The Spiritual Assembly concurred and recommended reinstatement. Morgan regained his administrative privileges.

He has remained dry for over twenty years. Many of Morgan's close friends, both Bahá'í and non-Bahá'í, have no idea of his struggle with alcoholism. In fact, Morgan has served the Bahá'í community with distinction for many years. He has been elected as delegate to the National Bahá'í Convention many times and has been elected and served on his Regional Council.

Morgan's story is a victory for both his personal growth and the patient, loving guidance and consolidation of the Bahá'í community and its institutions. The friends that knew of his difficulty treated him with love and respect throughout his ordeal. The Spiritual Assembly encouraged and assisted him for several years before it took administrative action that it felt was necessary.

The Spiritual Assembly's action, although a tough decision to make and a tough decision to receive, empowered Morgan to fight his spiritual battle and arise victorious like a Phoenix from the ashes of alcoholism. The love from his fellow believers shored up his courage throughout his struggle. He was enveloped by the bounties of God in his determination to acquire Bahá'í virtues and to live the Bahá'í life.

11
Transformation

As humanity passes through the age of transition in its evolution to a world civilisation which will be illuminated by spiritual values and will be distinguished by its justice and its unity, the role of the Baha'i community is clear: it must accomplish a spiritual transformation of its members, and must offer to the world a model of the society destined to come into being through the power of the Revelation of Baha'u'llah. From a letter written on behalf of the Universal House of Justice to an individual believer, 24th January 1993[55]

The spiritual transformation of the Bahá'ís and the Bahá'í community will witness new patterns of behavior and new vistas of thought and innovation. Throughout this book, stories of personal transformation have been described. In most cases, the power of friendship resulted in wonderful and sometimes miraculous change.

It has been my intent to demonstrate that the Fireside provides a core activity to transform our personal relations. The Fireside, as described by 'Abdu'l-Baha and Shoghi Effendi, suggests an intimate gathering in one's home. The opening of one's private domain invites the possibility of intimacy that society hungers for. Brotherhood and fellowship without intimacy is impossible to contemplate.

'Abdu'l-Baha in His visit to America in 1912 said that if only the friends would love one another, the city of New York would already have become Bahá'í. If that had happened in 1912 the world would have become completely transformed and perhaps a century of carnage could have been avoided. This isn't a condemnation of a past generation, it should be a rallying call to our generation.

In my years as a Bahá'í, every manner of teaching has been tried. I doubt that there are any revolutionary *silver bullets* left, but we seem to continue to look for them. We have all the tools for the conversion of mankind already at our disposal. The Guardian and the Master have said that the Fireside method of teaching is *perhaps the best method*. Perhaps we should go back to the suggestions of 'Abdu'l-Baha and Shoghi Effendi and try to do it that way.

The House of Justice has provided for us the tools to accompany the Fireside. The Study Circle guidance from the Continental Counselors in their June 1995 letter suggests a grassroots methodology of study that is a natural extension of the Fireside process:

> The initial organization of the INSTITUTE may consist of a small group of individuals around which a pattern of action develops...

> An approach to teaching INSTITUTES that is proving more successful is one that begins with a core group of experienced Baha'is and an evolving program for the spiritual education of the friends.

> ...the INSTITUTE, perhaps initially with little administrative machinery and simple program, but gradually developing the capacity to undertake more complex educational activities, would be assigned the task of the continuous education and deepening of the friends and of helping to raise up from among them those who would become devoted workers for the Cause and its avowed supporters.[56]

If we could only let go of the desire to focus on numbers and look at the process of transformation that the Fireside and Study Circles offer to us, we would be astonished to learn of the power latent within our communities if we would only arise.

Shoghi Effendi tells us, "this personal, informal, home teaching is perhaps the most productive of results."[57] I believe that the Fireside concept goes far beyond the immediate implication of swelling the ranks of believers. It can be the most transformative vehicle that we have for the spiritualization of the planet.

Active and successful teaching efforts through personal firesides will integrate with and fuel the momentum for growth outlined by the Universal House of Justice. The three core activities of study circles, devotional gatherings and children's classes could find their genesis and perhaps their growth in the growing intercourse between these complimentary and critical activities. Whether one begins with a fireside and then enters a study circle, or one begins with a study circle and then attends an intimate fireside gathering where his or her personal questions may be asked and studied, does not matter. What matters are the awakening, the growth and the development of a spiritual orientation in one's life.

> The coherence thus achieved through the establishment of study circles, devotional meetings and children's classes provides the initial impulse for growth in a cluster, an impulse that gathers strength as these core activities multiply in number.[58]

The Fireside requires from us to study the Writings; to open our homes for hospitality; to develop close and enduring friendships; and, to sharpen our sensitivities to the spiritual curiosity and inquiries of others. If the Bahá'í community worldwide could develop the competence of personal, individual Fireside teaching— small, intimate gatherings in one's home— on a scale not yet seen, coupled with an active participation in the three core activities, we could truly become the "leaven which leaveneth the world of being". [59]

> Philip was raised as a Nazi Youth. His father, whom he loved dearly, was a research librarian for the German SS. Although he was raised in this environment, his heart questioned certain aspects of what he was taught and after the war, as a teenager, he left his war-ravaged country and emigrated to the United States for school and a new life.
>
> Marie was a young woman in Denmark during World War II and spent her time assisting Jewish families escape the dark forces of the Nazi regime. She was caught by

the Germans and tortured by them to divulge the whereabouts of Jewish families. As she was being tortured, she prayed that if she were freed from this horror, she would dedicate her life to God and the service of humanity. The torture ceased and Marie spent the rest of the war in a camp—but survived.

Philip's aptitude for the sciences found a welcome encouragement at the campuses of the United States and he advanced as a highly successful nuclear scientist. He entered the workplace as a research scientist for General Electric and Westinghouse Nuclear development, married and had 3 children. His wife, Charlotte, after long-suffering from extreme bouts of depression, left him one day and never returned, leaving a young father to care for his 3 small children while attempting to keep his very demanding job. Philip was left confused, hurt and overwhelmed. He wondered how he was going to survive and care for his children. He wondered why life was the way it was and was there a purpose for all of this—the war, the extreme mental tests, the continuous struggle. Then he met Margie and Mel.

After the war, Marie worked ceaselessly to assist Jewish survivors to immigrate to Israel. Her work was so effective that she was honored by the new Israeli government and invited to Israel as an honored guest. While visiting the Holy Land, she was touring the beauty of this emerging new nation and was taken to the Bahá'í Gardens in Haifa. As she approached to entryway to the Gardens, the physical pain of her torture returned to her and she couldn't proceed. The flashback was as real as the events and Marie was taken to the hospital to rest. She left Israel shortly thereafter and immigrated to the United States. Her soul hungered for answers to why so much suffering was in the world and what was the purpose of her life. Then she met Margie and Mel.

Margie and Mel tried hard to invite someone to their home each week so that they could have an opportunity to speak about their beloved Bahá'í Faith. They would ask people to come and share the struggles they had in the quest for spiritual understanding and if the opportunity arose they would share some aspect of the Bahá'í Writings.

In the early 1970s, Marie immigrated to the town where Margie and Mel lived and met them at the grocery store. What a sweet and kind couple, she thought, as she watched them greet everyone in the store that they met with a kind word and a kind smile. Although they were shopping too, they seemed to know everyone and everyone seemed to know them too. Over a couple of weeks, Marie saw Margie and Mel several times in the grocery store and one day they struck up a very long conversation. Margie and Mel invited Marie to their home for dinner and to participate in a discussion they had each week on the spiritual purpose of life. Marie was attracted to both Margie and Mel and the idea of the discussion. She accepted.

Philip was transferred to a new job and moved himself and his 3 small children. It was difficult to start again in a new town, a new job and new schools for his children. He was lonely, felt sorry for himself and was becoming angry at the fate of his life and the world. But, Philip was really an optimist and he still looked for what was positive in life. While he was shopping at the small local grocery store, he met a vibrant couple that always greeted him with kindness. He found this refreshing as many people responded to him with suspicion because of his accent. Margie and Mel invited Philip to their home one evening for dinner and told him that they hosted a small discussion group about the meaning of life and our spiritual purpose. Philip was curious and delighted. However, he mentioned that he had 3 small children and couldn't accept. Margie told him that the children were welcome as well.

Over the course of the next several months, both Philip and Marie attended Margie and Mel's small fireside gathering. Occasionally someone else would come, but mostly it was just the four of them. What a curious gathering! Philip, the son of a German SS officer, and Marie, the victim of German SS torture. Over the course of that time, Philip and Marie grew into great friends. Marie took

Philip on as kind of a surrogate son and Philip looked at Marie as a parent who he missed terribly. Margie and Mel were delighted that these two wonderful souls were finding the healing they both needed so dearly in their friendship and their spiritual search.

One evening, Marie declared that she wanted to become a Bahá'í. Philip said that he wanted to as well. They both enrolled as Bahá'ís the same evening. They continued to study the Bahá'í Writings with Margie and Mel on a regular basis. As life would continue, the four close friends moved on to other places and other cities, but kept in touch.

Marie passed away a few years later. Years later, when Philip retired from his distinguished career, he decided to pioneer and serve his Faith in a foreign country. He decided that the only place that warmed his heart was to go to the home country of Marie and serve on her behalf to her countrymen. Philip left the United States and went to serve his beloved Faith for his dear friend. While there, he met and married. Philip and Marie and Margie and Mel will always be connected. Their lives were transformed by the friendship and fellowship that they found at the intimate fireside gathering that followed the instructions of their beloved Guardian.

Intimacy and friendship, fellowship and transformation is what humanity seeks and hungers for as it goes through the most turbulent time in the course of its maturing process. The Fireside, first demonstrated by the Blessed Bab, intimated throughout the Writings of the Blessed Beauty, Baha'u'llah, formulated and articulated through the tender guidance of Abdu'l-Baha, and expounded upon at length by the Sign of God on earth, Shoghi Effendi, provides the means for releasing the loving assistance from the Bahá'is to a grieving and anguished humanity. It provides a model for the future interactions of community life—hospitality, intimate discussion, spiritual discourse and discovery, and, personal and community transformation.

> The field is indeed so immense, the period so critical, the Cause so great, the workers so few, the time so short, the privilege so priceless, that no follower of the Faith of Baha'u'llah, worthy to bear His name, can afford a moment's hesitation. That God-born Force, irresistible in its sweeping power, incalculable in its potency, unpredictable in its course, mysterious in its workings, and awe-inspiring in its manifestations--a Force which, as the Bab has written, "vibrates within the innermost being of all created things," and which, according to Baha'u'llah, has through its "vibrating influence," "upset the equilibrium of the world and revolutionized its ordered life"-- such a Force, acting even as a two-edged sword, is, under our very eyes, sundering, on the one hand, the age-old ties which for centuries have held together the fabric of civilized society, and is unloosing, on the other, the bonds that still fetter the infant and as yet unemancipated Faith of Baha'u'llah. The

undreamt-of opportunities offered through the operation of this Force--the American believers must now rise, and fully and courageously exploit them. "The holy realities of the Concourse on high," writes Abdu'l-Baha, "yearn, in this day, in the Most Exalted Paradise, to return unto this world, so that they may be aided to render some service to the threshold of the Abha Beauty, and arise to demonstrate their servitude to His sacred Threshold." Shoghi Effendi, *The Advent of Divine Justice*, p. 47[60]

1. Make Many Contacts

- What is a contact?
- How do I make a contact?
- List 15 contacts

2. Select a few who they feel would become Baha'is

- What do we mean by "select"?
- How do I know if someone "would become a Baha'i"?
- List 5 of my contacts who "would become a Baha'i" and why do I think so
  - •
  - •
  - •
  - •
  - •

3. Develop a Close Friendship with them

- Who are my close friends?
- What makes them "close"?
- How did I become close with them?
- Identify 3 things that I could do with one of my contacts (that I think could become a Baha'i) to become close

4. Then Complete Confidence

- What does it mean to have confidence with someone?
- How do I complete confidence with someone?

5. Finally Teach them the Cause

- How might I teach each contact?

6. Until they become Strong

- What is my role in the teaching and consolidating my contacts?

Appendix 2
Additional Quotes from the Writings

I. The Individual

Not by the force of numbers, not by the mere exposition of a set of new and noble principles, not by an organized campaign of teaching—no matter how worldwide and elaborate in its character—not even by the staunchness of our faith or the exaltation of our enthusiasm, can we ultimately hope to vindicate in the eyes of a critical and sceptical age the supreme claim of the Abha Revelation. One thing and only one thing will unfailingly and alone secure the undoubted triumph of this sacred Cause, namely, the extent to which our own inner life and private character mirror forth in their manifold aspects the splendor of those eternal principles proclaimed by Baha'u'llah.

(Shoghi Effendi, *Bahá'í Administration*, page 66)

It is primarily a task that concerns the individual believer, wherever he may be, and whatever his calling, his resources, his race, or his age. Neither the local nor national representatives of the community, no matter how elaborate their plans, or persistent their appeals, or sagacious their counsels, nor even the Guardian himself, however much he may yearn for this consummation, can decide where the duty of the individual lies, or supplant him in the discharge of that task. The individual alone must assess its character, consult his conscience, prayerfully consider all its aspects, manfully struggle against the natural inertia that weighs him down in his effort to arise, shed, heroically and irrevocably, the trivial and superfluous attachments which hold him back, empty himself of every thought that may tend to obstruct his path, mix, in obedience to the counsels of the Author of His Faith, and in imitation of the One Who is its true Exemplar, with men and women, in all walks of life, seek to touch their hearts, through the distinction which characterizes his thoughts, his words and his acts, and win them over tactfully, lovingly, prayerfully and persistently, to the Faith he himself has espoused.

(Shoghi Effendi, *Citadel of Faith*, page 148)

The role of the individual is of unique importance in the work of the Cause. It is the individual who manifests the vitality of faith upon which the success of the teaching work and the development of the community depend. Baha'u'llah's command to each believer to teach His Faith confers an inescapable responsibility which cannot be transferred to, or assumed by, any institution of the Cause. The individual alone can exercise those capacities which include the ability to take initiative, to seize opportunities, to form friendships, to interact personally with others, to build relationships, to win the cooperation of others in common service to the Faith and society, and to convert into action the decisions made by consultative bodies. It is the individual's duty to "consider every avenue of approach which he might utilize in his personal attempts to capture the attention, maintain the interest, and deepen the faith, of those whom he seeks to bring into the fold of his Faith."

To optimize the use of these capacities, the individual draws upon his love for Baha'u'llah, the power of the Covenant, the dynamics of prayer, the inspiration and education derived from regular reading and study of the Holy Texts, and the transformative forces that operate upon his soul as he strives to behave in accordance with the divine laws and principles. In addition to these, the individual, having been given the duty to teach the Cause, is endowed with the capacity to attract particular blessings promised by Baha'u'llah. "Whoso openeth his lips in this Day," the Blessed Beauty asserts, "and maketh mention of the name of his Lord, the hosts of Divine inspiration shall descend upon him from the heaven of My name, the All-Knowing, the All-Wise. On him shall also descend the Concourse on high, each bearing aloft a chalice of pure light."

Shoghi Effendi underscored the absolute necessity of individual initiative and action. He explained that without the support of the individual, "at once wholehearted, continuous and generous," every measure and plan of his National Spiritual Assembly is "foredoomed to failure," the purpose of the Master's Divine Plan is "impeded"; furthermore, the sustaining strength of Baha'u'llah Himself "will be withheld from every and each individual who fails in the long run to arise and play his part." Hence, at the very crux of any progress to be made is the individual believer, who possesses the power of execution which only he can release through his own initiative and sustained action. Regarding the sense of inadequacy that sometimes hampers individual initiative, a letter written on his behalf conveys the Guardian's advice: "Chief among these, you mention the lack of courage and of initiative on the part of the believers, and a feeling of inferiority which prevents them from addressing the public. It is precisely these weaknesses that he wishes the friends to overcome, for these do not only paralyse their efforts but actually serve to quench the flame of faith in their hearts. Not until all the friends come to realize that every one of them is able, in his own measure, to deliver the Message, can they ever hope to reach the goal that has been set before them by a loving and wise Master.... Everyone is a potential teacher. He has only to use what God has given him and thus prove that he is faithful to his trust."

(The Universal House of Justice, Ridvan 153 B.E. (World))

...In so responding, each individual, too, must make a conscious decision as to what he or she will do to serve the Plan, and as to how, where and when to do it. This determination enables the individual to check the progress of his actions and, if necessary, to modify the steps being taken. Becoming accustomed to such a procedure of systematic striving lends meaning and fulfilment to the life of any Baha'i.

But beyond the necessity of responding to the call of the institutions, the individual is charged by Baha'u'llah Himself with the sacred duty of teaching His Cause, described by Him as the "most meritorious of all deeds. "So long as there are souls in need of enlightenment, this duty must surely remain the constant occupation of every believer. In its fulfilment, the individual is directly responsible to Baha'u'llah. "Let him not wait for any directions," Shoghi Effendi urgently advises, "or expect any special encouragement, from the elected representatives of his community, nor be deterred by any obstacles which his relatives, or fellow-citizens may be inclined to place in his path, nor mind the censure of his critics or enemies." The writings of the Central Figures and of our Guardian are replete with advice and exhortations concerning the individual's irreplaceable role in the advancement of the Cause. So it is inevitable that we should feel impelled, at this particular time in the life of humanity as a whole, to appeal directly to each member of our community to ponder the urgent situation facing us all as the helpers of the Abha Beauty.

(The Universal House of Justice, Ridvan 155 B.E.)

II. How Do We Personally Prepare?

Be ye loving fathers to the orphan, and a refuge to the helpless, and a treasury for the poor, and a cure for the ailing. Be ye the helpers of every victim of oppression, the patrons of the disadvantaged. Think ye at all times of rendering some service to every member of the human race. Pay ye no heed to aversion and rejection, to disdain, hostility, injustice: act ye in the opposite way. Be ye sincerely kind, not in appearance only. Let each one of God's loved ones centre his attention on this: to be the Lord's mercy to man; to be the Lord's grace. Let him do some good to every person whose path he crosseth, and be of some benefit to him. Let him improve the character of each and all, and reorient the minds of men. In this way, the light of divine guidance will shine forth, and the blessings of God will cradle all mankind: for love is light, no matter in what abode it dwelleth; and hate is darkness, no matter where it may make its nest. O friends of God! That the hidden Mystery may stand revealed, and the secret essence of all things may be disclosed, strive ye to banish that darkness for ever and ever.

(Abdu'l Baha, *Selections From the Writings of Abdu'l Baha*, page 3)

To strive to obtain a more adequate understanding of the significance of 'Baha'u'llah's stupendous Revelation must, it is my unalterable conviction, remain the first obligation and the object of the constant endeavor of each one of its loyal adherents. An exact and thorough comprehension of so vast a system, so sublime a revelation, so sacred a trust, is for obvious reasons beyond the reach and ken of our finite minds. We can, however, and it is our bounden duty to seek to derive fresh inspiration and added sustenance as we labor for the propagation of His Faith through a clearer apprehension of the truths it enshrines and the principles on which it is based.

(Shoghi Effendi, *World Order of Baha'u'llah*, page 100)

In their efforts to achieve this purpose they must study for themselves, conscientiously and painstakingly, the literature of their Faith, delve into its teachings, assimilate its laws and principles, ponder its admonitions, tenets and purposes, commit to memory certain of its exhortations and prayers, master the essentials of its administration, and keep abreast of its current affairs and latest developments. They must strive to obtain, from sources that are authoritative and unbiased, a sound knowledge of the history and tenets of Islam--the source and background of their Faith--and approach reverently and with a mind purged from preconceived ideas the study of the Qur'an which, apart from the sacred scriptures of the 'Babi and 'Baha'i Revelations, constitutes the only Book which can be regarded as an absolutely authenticated Repository of the Word of God. They must devote special attention to the investigation of those institutions and circumstances that are directly connected with the origin and birth of their Faith, with the station claimed by its Forerunner, and with the laws revealed by its Author.

(Shoghi Effendi, *Advent of Divine Justice*, page 50)

First and foremost one should resort to every possible means to purge one's heart and motives, otherwise it would be futile t engage in any form of enterprise. It is also essential to abstain from hypocrisy and blind imitation, inasmuch as their foul odor would soon be detected by every man of understanding and wisdom. Moreover the friends must observe the specific times for the remembrance of God, meditation, devotion, and prayer, as it is highly unlikely, nay, rather impossible, that any enterprise should prosper and develop short of divine bestowals and confirmation. One can hardly imagine what a great influence genuine love, truthfulness and purity of motives exert on the souls of men. But these traits cannot be acquired unless every believer makes a daily effort to gain them...

It is primarily through the potency of noble deeds and character, then by the power of exposition and proofs that the friends of God should demonstrate to the world the fact that what has been promised by God is bound to happen, that it is already taking place and that the divine glad-tidings are clear, evident and complete.

(From a letter dated 19 December 1923 written by Shoghi Effendi to the Bahá'is of the East)

III. What is a Fireside?

The friends of God should weave bonds of fellowship with others and show absolute love and affection towards them. These links have a deep influence on people and they will listen. When the friends sense receptivity to the Word of God, they should deliver the Message with wisdom. They must first try and remove any apprehensions in the people they teach. In fact, every one of the believers should choose one person every year and try to establish ties of friendship with him, so that all his fear would disappear. Only then, and gradually, must he teach that person. This is the best method.

('Abdu'l-Bahá, From a Tablet- translated from the Persian)
The world of humanity is filled with darkness; you are its radiant candles. It is very poor; you must be the treasury of the Kingdom. It is exceedingly debased; you must be the cause of its exaltation. It is bereft of divine graces; you must give it impetus and spiritual quickening. According to the teachings of Baha'u'llah you must love and cherish each individual member of humanity.

('Abdu'l-Bahá, *The Promulgation of Universal Peace,* page 337)

The believers must be encouraged to teach individually in their own homes. Baha'u'llah has enjoined upon the Baha'is the sacred obligation of teaching. We have no priests, therefore the service once rendered by priests to their religions is the service every single Baha'i is expected to render individually to his religion. He must be the one who enlightens new souls, confirms them, heals the wounded and the weary upon the road of life, and gives them to quaff from the chalice of everlasting life the knowledge of the Manifestation of God in His Day.

(From a letter dated 5 July 1957 written on behalf of Shoghi Effendi to the National Spiritual Assembly of Benelux countries)

IV. Why is a Fireside so important?

Teaching the Cause of God is not only through the tongue; it is through deeds, a good disposition, happiness of nature, kindness and sympathy, good fellowship, trustworthiness, holiness, virtue, purity of ideals, and lastly, speech.

('Abdu'l-Bahá: Bahá'i News, No. 243, May 1951, page 8)

Let him refrain, at the outset, from insisting on such laws and observances as might impose too severe a strain on the seeker's newly-awakened faith, and endeavor to nurse him, patiently, tactfully, and yet determinedly into full maturity, and aid him to proclaim his unqualified acceptance of whatever has been ordained by Baha'u'llah. Let him, as soon as that stage has been attained, introduce him to the body of his fellow-believers, and seek through constant fellowship and active participation in the local activities of his community, to enable him to contribute his share to the enrichment of its life, the furtherance of its tasks, the consolidation of its interests, and the coordination of its activities with those of its sister communities. Let him not be content until he has infused into his spiritual child so deep a longing as to impel him to arise independently, in his turn, and devote his energies to the quickening of other souls, and the upholding of the laws and principles laid down by his newly-adopted faith.

(Shoghi Effendi, *The Advent of Divine Justice*, page 42)

The Guardian feels that the most effective way for the Bahá'is to teach the Faith is to make strong friends with their neighbors and associates. When the friends have confidence in the Bahá'is and the Bahá'is in their friends, they should give the Message and teach the Cause. Individual teaching of this type is more effective than any other type...

(From a letter dated 27 December 1954 written on behalf of Shoghi Effendi to an individual believer)

It should not be overlooked, however, that the most powerful and effective teaching medium that has been found so far is the fireside meeting, because in the fireside meeting, intimate personal questions can be answered, and the student find the spirit of the Faith more abundant there.

(From a letter dated 11 December 1952 written on behalf of Shoghi Effendi to a Local Spiritual Assembly and an individual believer)

The most effective method of teaching is the Fireside group, where new people can be shown Baha'i hospitality, and ask all questions which bother them. They can feel there the true Baha'i spirit—and it is the spirit that quickeneth.

(From a letter dated 20 October 1956 written on behalf of Shoghi Effendi to an individual believer)

The Guardian hopes the Friends ... will display the loving spirit of the Master in their contacts, and then win those souls to the Faith. The fireside method of teaching seems to produce the greatest results, when each one invites friends into their homes once in nineteen days, and introduces them to the Faith. Close association and loving service affects the hearts; and when the heart is affected, then the spirit can enter. It is the Holy Spirit that quickens, and the Friends must become channels for its diffusion.

(From a letter dated 27 January 1957 written on behalf of Shoghi Effendi to an individual believer)

V. What is the Fireside Method of Teaching?

The Baha'is must realize that the success of this work depends upon the individual. The individual must arise as never before to proclaim the Faith of Baha'u'llah. The most effective way for them to carry on their work is for the individual to make many contacts, select a few who they feel would become Baha'is, develop a close friendship with them, then complete confidence, and finally teach them the Faith, until they become strong supporters of the Cause of God.

(Prom a letter dated 13 May 1955 written on behalf of Shoghi Effendi to all NSAs)

The believers are entirely free to hold as many little teaching groups or Firesides as they please in their own homes... In fact this personal, informal, home teaching is perhaps the most productive of results.

(From a letter dated 24 February 1950 written on behalf of Shoghi Effendi to an individual believer)

References

Introduction
1. Shoghi Effendi, *The World Order Of Bahá'u'lláh*, p. 42.
2. `Abdu'l-Bahá, as quoted in *The Individual and Teaching: Raising the Divine Call*, p. 12.
3. Rúhíyyih Rabbaní, *The Priceless Pearl*, p.

Chapter 1
4. Shoghi Effendi, Bahá'í *Administration*, pg. 66.

Chapter 2
5. Shoghi Effendi, *Advent of Divine Justice*, pg. 46.
6. The Universal House of Justice, *Ridvan Message 153 B.E.*, paragraph 22.
7. The Universal House of Justice, *Ridvan 153 B.E.*, paragraph 22.
8. `Abdu'l-Bahá, *Abdu'l Bahá in London*, pg 127
9. `Abdu'l-Bahá, *Promulgation of Universal Peace*, pg 219
10. Shoghi Effendi, The Light Of Divine Guidance. Vol. 1, p. 108.
11. The Universal House of Justice, *Ridvan 153 B.E.*, paragraph 20.
12. Bahá'u'lláh, *The Hidden Words Of Bahá'u'lláh*, p. 4,
13. Bahá'u'lláh, *Gleanings*, pg 315
14. Bahá'u'lláh, *Kitáb-i-Aqdas: The Most Holy Book*, Introduction, p. 1.
15. Shoghi Effendi, *Promise Day is Come, p. 121.*

16. Bahá'u'lláh, as quoted in *Education, Compilation of Compilations*, Vol I, no. 6.
17. Bahá'u'lláh, *Kitáb-i-Aqdas: The Most Holy Book*, K5, p. 21.
18. `Abdu'l-Bahá, *Selections from the Writings of `Abdu'l-Bahá*, sec. 209, p. 264.
19. The Universal House of Justice, *Ridvan Message 153 B.E.*, paragraph 21.

Chapter 3
20. Shoghi Effendi, *World Order of Bahá'u'lláh*, p. 100.
21. The Universal House of Justice, *Ridvan Message 153 B.E.*, paragraph 21.
22. Bahá'u'lláh, *Kitáb-i-Aqdas: The Most Holy Book*, K182, p.85.
23. Bahá'u'lláh, *The Hidden Words*, no. 31, p. 11.
24. Bahá'u'lláh, *The Kitáb -i-Ígán: The Book of Certitude*, p. 238.
25. `Abdu'l-Bahá, *LSA Guidelines*, Chapter 4, p. 11.
26. The Universal House of Justice, *Ridvan Message 153 B.E.*, paragraph 21

Chapter 4
27. `Abdu'l-Bahá, as quoted in *Guidelines for Teaching, Compilations of Compilations*, Vol. II, no. 1924. .
28. Shoghi Effendi, as quoted in *Guidelines for Teaching, Compilations of Compilations*, Vol. II, no. 2000
29. *ibid*, no. 2005.
30. *The Dawn Breakers*, p. 52-61.
31. Shoghi Effendi, as quoted in *Guidelines for Teaching, Compilations of Compilations*, Vol. II, no. 1983.

32. Bahá'u'lláh, *Tablets of Bahá'u'lláh*, p. 196.
33. Bahá'u'lláh, *The Hidden Words* (from the Persian), no. 36.
34. Queen Marie of Romania, as quoted in *God Passes By*, p. 389.
35. Shoghi Effendi, as quoted in *Guidelines for Teaching, Compilations of Compilations*, Vol. II, no. 1991.
36. *ibid*, no. 2005

Chapter 5
37. Bahá'u'lláh, *Gleanings from the Writings of Bahá'u'lláh*, p. 289.
38. `Abdu'l-Bahá, *Tablets of `Abdu'l-Bahá*, p. 219-20.

Chapter 6
39. `Abdu'l-Bahá, *Selections from the Writings of `Abdu'l-Bahá*, p. 269.
40. The Bible, *Ecclesiastes 4:2*.
41. The Intimacy Game

Chapter 7
42. `Abdu'l-Bahá, as quoted in *The Individual and Teaching: Raising the Divine Call*, p. 37.
43. Bahá'u'lláh, *Tablets of Bahá'u'lláh*, p. 35.
44. `Abdu'l-Bahá, *Paris Talks*, p. 181.
45. Bahá'u'lláh, as quoted in *Crisis and Victory, Compilations of Compilations*, Vol. I, p. 155.
46. Shoghi Effendi, *The Advent of Divine Justice*, p. 53.
47. ibid.

Chapter 8
48. `Abdu'l-Bahá, *The Promulgation of Universal Peace*, p. 256.

49. Shoghi Effendi, as quoted in *Guidelines for Teaching, Compilations of Compilations*, Vol. II, no. 1991.
50. `Abdu'l-Bahá, Prayer for Marriage, *Bahá'í Prayers*, p. 106.

Chapter 9
51. Shoghi Effendi, as quoted in *The Individual and Teaching: Raising the Divine Call*, p. 37.

Chapter 10
52. The Universal House of Justice, from a letter, dated 3 November 1974, to a National Spiritual Assembly, in an unpublished compilation prepared by the International Teaching Center.
53. The Universal House of Justice, *Entry by Troops, Compilations of Compilations*, Vol. I, p. 11.
54. Shoghi Effendi, *The Advent of Divine Justice*, p. 52.

Chapter 11
55. The Universal House of Justice, from a letter written on behalf of the Universal House of Justice to an individual believer on Violence and Sexual Abuse of Women and Children, 24 Janauary, 1993.
56. Synopsis of the Institute Training Program's letter prepared at the Bahá'í World Center for the International Teaching Center dated June 1995.
57. Shoghi Effendi, as quoted in *Guidelines for Teaching, Compilations of Compilations*, Vol. II, no. 1974.
58. The Universal House of Justice, *Building Momentum: A Coherent Approach to Growth*, p. 9.

59. Bahá'u'lláh, *Gleanings from the Writings of Bahá'u'lláh*, p. 157.
60. Shoghi Effendi, *The Advent of Divine Justice*, p. 47.

Appendix 2
61. Shoghi Effendi, *Bahá'í Administration*, p. 66.
62. Shoghi Effendi, *Citadel of Faith*, p. 148.
63. The Universal House of Justice, *Ridvan Message 153 B.E.*, paragraphs 20-22.
64. The Universal House of Justice, *Ridvan Message 155 B.E.*, paragraphs 13-14.
65. Shoghi Effendi, *World Order of Bahá'u'lláh*, p. 100.
66. Shoghi Effendi, From a letter dated 19 December 1923 written by Shoghi Effendi to the Bahá'ís of the East.
67. `Abdu'l-Bahá, *Selections from the Writings of `Abdu'l-Bahá*, p. 3.
68. Shoghi Effendi, *The Advent of Divine Justice*, p. 50.
69. Shoghi Effendi, as quoted in *Guidelines for Teaching, Compilations of Compilations, Vol. II, no. 2009*.
70. `Abdu'l-Bahá, , as quoted in *Guidelines for Teaching, Compilations of Compilations, Vol. II, no. 1924*
71. `Abdu'l-Bahá, *The Promulgation of Universal Peace*, p. 337.
72. `Shoghi Effendi, , as quoted in *Guidelines for Teaching, Compilations of Compilations, Vol. II, no. 1987*.
73. *ibid*, no. 1983.
74. *ibid*, no. 2000.

75. *ibid*, no. 2005.
76. *ibid*, no. 1991.
77. *ibid*, no. 1974.
78. Shoghi Effendi, *The Advent of Divine Justice*, p. 42.
79. `Abdu'l-Bahá, *Bahá'í News*, No. 243, May 1951, p. 8.

Bibliography

--------- `Abdu'l-Bahá. `*Abdu'l-Bahá in London: Addresses and Notes of Conversations*. London: Bahá'í Publishing Trust, 1982.

--------- *The Bahá'í News*, No. 243, May 1951, Wilmette, Ill.: Bahá'í Publishing Trust, 1951.

--------- *Paris Talks: Addresses Given by `Abdu'l-Bahá in Paris in 1911*. 11th ed. London: Bahá'í Publishing Trust, 1972.

--------- *The Promulgation of Universal Peace: Talks Delivered by `Abdu'l-Bahá during His Vist to the United States and Canada in 1912*. Compiled by Howard MacNutt. 2nd ed. Wilmette, Ill.: Bahá'í Publishing Trust, 1982.

--------- *Selections from the Writings of `Abdu'l-Bahá*. Compiled by the Research Department of the Universal House of Justice. Translated by a Committee at the Bahá'í World Center and Marzieh Gail. Haifa: Bahá'í World Center, 1982.

--------- *Tablets of `Abdu'l-Bahá*. 3 vols. New York: Bahá'í Publishing Trust, 1977.

--------- *Bahá'i Prayers*, New York: Bahá'i Publishing Trust, 1984.

--------- Bahá'u'lláh. *Gleanings from the Writings of Bahá'u'lláh*. 2nd ed. Translated by Shoghi Effendi. Wilmette, Ill.: Bahá'í Publishing Trust, 1990.

--------- *The Hidden Words of Bahá'u'lláh*. Translated by Shoghi Effendi. Wilmette, Ill.: Bahá'í Publishing Trust, 1985

--------- *The Kitáb-i-*Aqdas: *The Most Holy Book*. Compiled by the Universal House of Justice with the assistance of a Committee at the Bahá'í World Centre. Haifa, Bahá'í World Center, 1992.

--------- *The Kitáb -i-Ígán: The Book of Certitude*. 2nd ed. Translated by Shoghi Effendi. Wilmette, Ill.: Bahá'í Publishing Trust, 1989.

--------- *Tablets of Bahá'u'lláh Revealed after the Kitáb-i-*Aqdas. Compiled by the research Department of the Universal House of Justice, translated by Habib Taherzadeh with the assistance of a Committee at the Bahá'í World Centre. Bahá'í Publishing Trust, Wilmette, Ill.: 1988.

--------- Bahá'u'lláh, `Abdu'l-Bahá, and Shoghi Effendi. *Crisis and Victory: Compilation of Compilations*, Vol I, Compiled by the Research Department of the Universal House of Justice, Bahá'í Publications Australia, revised 1990.

--------- *Education, Compilation of Compilations*, Vol I, Compiled by the Research Department of the Universal House of Justice, Bahá'í Publications Australia, revised 1990.

--------- *Entry by Troops, Compilation of Compilations*, Vol I, Compiled by the Research Department of the Universal House of Justice, Bahá'í Publications Australia, revised 1990.

--------- *Guidelines for Teaching, Compilation of Compilations*, Vol II, Compiled by the Research Department of the Universal House of Justice, Bahá'í Publications Australia, revised 1990.

--------- *Teaching the Masses, Compilation of Compilations*, Vol II, Compiled by the Research Department of the Universal House of Justice, Bahá'í Publications Australia, revised 1990.

--------- Bahá'u'lláh, The Bab, and `Abdu'l-Bahá. *Bahá'í Prayers: A Selection of the Prayers Revealed by Bahá'u'lláh, The Bab, and `Abdu'l-Bahá*. Wilmette, Ill.: Bahá'í Publishing Trust, 1970.

--------- *The Bible.* The Authorized King James Version.

--------- *The Dawn Breakers, Nabíl's Narrative of the Early Days of the Bahá'í Revelation*, New York, Bahá'í Publishing Trust, Wilmette, 1970.

-------- *Developing Distinctive* Bahá'í *Communities: Guidelines for Spiritual Assemblies*, National Spiritual Assembly of the Bahá'í s of the United States, Office of Assembly Development, Evanston, National Spiritual Assembly of the Bahá'í of the United States, 1998.

-------- Institute Training Program, *Synposis of the Institute Training Programs letter*, Haifa, Israel. Bahá'í World Center, June 1995.

-------- Rúhíyyih Rabbaní. *The Priceless Pearl.* Britian, Bahá'í Publishing Trust, 1969.

-------- Shoghi Effendi. *The Advent of Divine Justice.* Wilmette, Ill.: Bahá'í Publishing Trust, 1990.

-------- Bahá'í *Administration: Selected Messages 1922-1932.* 7th rev. ed. Wilmette, Ill.: Bahá'í Publishing Trust, 1974.

-------- *Citadel of Faith: Messages to America 1947-1957.* Wilmette, Ill.: Bahá'í Publishing Trust, 1981.

-------- *God Passes By.* Wilmette, Ill.: Bahá'í Publishing Trust, rev. ed., 1974.

-------- From a letter dated 19 December 1923 written by Shoghi Effendi to the Bahá'ís of the East.

-------- *The Light of Divine Guidance: The Messages from the Guardian of the Bahá'í Faith to the Bahá'ís of Germany and Austria.* Hofheim-Langenhain: Bahá'í-Verlag, 1982.

--------- *The Promised Day is Come*. 3rd ed. Wilmette, Ill.: Bahá'í Publishing Trust, 1980.

--------- *The World Order of Bahá'u'lláh: Selected Letters.* 2nd ed. Wilmette, Ill.: Bahá'í Publishing Trust, 1991.

--------- The Universal House of Justice. From a letter written on behalf of the Universal House of Justice to an individual believer on Violence and Sexual Abuse of Women and Children, 24 Janauary, 1993.

-------- from a letter, dated 3 November 1974, to a National Spiritual Assembly, in an unpublished compilation prepared by the International Teaching Center. Haifa, Israel.

--------- *The Ridvan Message: 153 B.E (1993)*. Haifa, Bahá'í World Center, 1993.

--------- *The Ridvan Message: 155 B.E (1995)*. Haifa, Bahá'í World Center, 1995.

--------- *The Individual and Teaching: Raising the Divine Call*.